Also by Amity Shlaes

Germany: The Empire Within

THE
GREEDY
HAND

THE

GREEDY

HAND

How **TAXES**
Drive Americans Crazy
and What to Do About It

Amity Shlaes

RANDOM HOUSE

NEW YORK

Library of Congress Cataloging-in-Publication Data
Shlaes, Amity.
The greedy hand: how taxes drive Americans crazy and what to do about it/Amity Shlaes.
p.   cm.
Includes index.
ISBN 0-375-50132-0
1. Taxation—United States. 2. Taxation—Law and legislation—United States. I. Title.
HJ2362.S54   1999   336.2'00973—dc21   98-31243

Random House website address: www.atrandom.com

2   4   6   8   9   7   5   3

First Edition

Book design by Mercedes Everett

Again, for Seth

If, from the more wretched parts of the old world, we look at those which are in an advanced stage of improvement, we still find the greedy hand of government thrusting itself into every corner and crevice of industry, and grasping the spoil of the multitude. Invention is continually exercised, to furnish new pretenses for revenues and taxation. It watches prosperity as its prey and permits none to escape without tribute.

—Thomas Paine,
Rights of Man, Introduction to Part the Second

Contents

THE
GREEDY
HAND

1

THE GREEDY HAND

THE FATHER OF THE MODERN AMERICAN STATE WAS A
pipe-puffing executive at R. H. Macy & Co. named Beardsley Ruml. Ruml, the department store's treasurer, also
served as chairman of the board of directors of the Federal
Reserve Bank of New York and advisor to President
Franklin Roosevelt during World War II. In those years
Washington was busy marshaling the forces of the American economy to halt Japan and Germany. In 1942, not long
after Pearl Harbor, lawmakers raised income taxes radically, with rates that aimed to capture twice as much revenue as in the previous year. They also imposed the income
tax on tens of millions of Americans who had never been acquainted with the levy before. The change was so dramatic
that the chroniclers of that period have coined a phrase to
describe it. They say that the "class tax" became a "mass tax."

The new rates were law. But Americans were ill-prepared to face a new and giant tax bill. A Gallup poll
from the period showed that only some 5 million of the
34 million people who were subject to the tax for the
first time were saving to make their payment. In those

days, March 15, not April 15, was the nation's annual tax deadline.

The Treasury nervously launched a huge public relations campaign to remind Americans of their new duties. A Treasury Department poster exhorted citizens: "You are one of 50,000,000 Americans who must fill out an income tax form by March 15. DO IT NOW!" For wartime theatergoers, Disney had prepared an animated short film featuring citizen Donald Duck laboring over his tax return beside a bottle of aspirin. Donald claimed exemptions and dependent credits for Huey, Dewey, and Louie.

As March 15, 1943 neared, though, it became clear that many citizens still were not filing returns. Henry Morgenthau, the Treasury secretary, confronted colleagues about the nightmarish prospect of mass tax evasion: "Suppose we have to go out and try to arrest five million people?"

The Macy's Model

Enter Ruml, man of ideas. At Macy's, he had observed that customers didn't like big bills. They preferred making payments bit by bit, in the installment plan, even if they had to pay for the pleasure with interest. So Ruml devised a plan, which he unfolded to his colleagues at the Federal Reserve and to anyone in Washington who would listen. The government would get business to do its work, collecting taxes for it. Employers would retain a percentage of taxes from workers every week—say, 20 percent—and forward it directly to Washington's war chest. This would hide the size of the new taxes from the worker. No longer would the worker ever have to look his tax bill square in the eye.

Workers need never even see the money they were forgoing. Withholding as we know it today was born.

This was more than change, it was transformation. Government would put its hand into the taxpayer's pocket and grab its share of tax—without asking.

Ruml hadn't invented withholding. His genius was to make its introduction palatable by adding a powerful sweetener: the federal government would offer a tax amnesty for the previous year, allowing confused and indebted citizens to start on new footing. It was the most ambitious bait-and-switch plan in America's history.

Ruml advertised his project as a humane effort to smooth life in the disruption of the war. He noted it was a way to help taxpayers out of the habit of carrying income tax debt, debt that he characterized as "a pernicious fungus permeating the structure of things." The move was also patriotic. At Macy's, executives had found that a "young man in the comptroller's office who was making $75 or $100 [a week was] called into the navy at a salary of $2,600 and we had to get together and take care of his income tax for him." The young man, Ruml saw, would face a tax bill for a higher income at a time when he was earning less money in the service of his country. This Ruml deemed "an impossible situation."

Ruml had several reasons for wagering that his project would work. One was that Americans, smarting from the Japanese assault, were now willing to sacrifice more than at any other point in memory. The second was that the federal government would be able to administer withholding—six successful years of Social Security showed that the government, for the first time ever, was able to handle such a mass program of revenue collection. The third was packaging.

He called his program not "collection at source" or "withholding," two technical terms for what he was doing. Instead he chose a zippier name: "pay as you go." And most important of all, there was the lure of the tax amnesty.

The policy thinkers of the day embraced the Ruml arrangement. This was an era in which John Maynard Keynes dominated the world of economics. The Keynesians placed enormous faith in government. The one thing they liked about the war was that it demonstrated to the world all the miracles that Big Government could work. The Ruml plan would give them the wherewithal to have their projects even, they sensed, after the war ended. Keynesianism also said high taxes were crucial to controlling inflation. The Keynesians saw withholding as the right tool for getting those necessary high taxes.

Conservatives played their part in the drama. Among withholding's backers was the man who was later to become the world's leading free-market economist, Milton Friedman. Decades after the war, Friedman called for the abolition of the withholding system. In his memoirs he wrote that "we concentrated single-mindedly on promoting the war effort. We gave next to no consideration to any longer-run consequences. It never occurred to me at the time that I was helping to develop machinery that would make possible a government that I would come to criticize severely as too large, too instrusive, too destructive of freedom. Yet, that was precisely what I was doing." With an almost audible sigh, Friedman added: "There is an important lesson here. It is far easier to introduce a government program than to get rid of it."

Such questions, though, had no place in the mind of a nation under attack. At the moment what seemed most important was that voters accepted the Ruml plan. Randolph Paul, a Treasury Department official and Ruml critic, wrote resignedly that "his plan had political appeal. Though he conceived the plan as getting people out of debt to the government, the public thought that Ruml had found a very white rabbit"—a magic trick—"which would somehow lighten their tax load."

The Amnesty Ruse

Congress got to work. Ruml followers joined hands. The Rumlites, as they were known, succeeded in passing a version of the Ruml plan. "The Current Tax Payment Act of 1943" included the only full-fledged federal amnesty on personal income taxes to take place this century, granting taxpayers forgiveness of 75 percent of the lower of a taxpayer's 1942 or 1943 liabilities. The ruse was on.

"Pay as you go" became the rule nationwide in July of 1943, or in the same weeks as Allied Forces landed on Sicily. Workers suddenly began receiving 20 percent less in their paychecks. "This amount is not a new tax," assured the Treasury in a breathless letter distributed to forestall panic. "[It is] in payment of your regular Federal Income and Victory Tax." The Treasury chose the same moment to inform Americans of a new piece of paper that would now enter their lives, the ancestor of today's W-2's: "After the close of the year your employer will give you a receipt showing exactly how much of your money has gone to the United States Treasury toward the payment of your taxes. Keep that receipt. It is your evidence of taxes paid."

At the time the whole arrangement was presented as just another contingency step taken in the extraordinary fight against the Nazis. But even in the mêlée of those war years it became clear that a new page was being written in the annals of public finance. America was a nation born of a tax revolt. For the first century of the country's history, its people and courts had rejected the income tax altogether. Yet here, after withholding, the planners' hopes were being borne out. It seemed that the average citizen really was willing to accept high taxes, as long as they were buried in a program like "pay as you go."

Now the big thinkers began to dream. Withholding would indeed do more than fund the occupation of Germany or victory over Japan. As 1943 and 1944 passed, with taxpayers obediently accepting their smaller checks, they got to work on the blueprints of their postwar projects. These were years in which everyone feared a return of the Depression. With the Ruml plan in service, they believed, they could spend their way out of future economic trouble. Emboldened by his own successes, Ruml himself compiled lists of new uses for federal taxes, among them to control inflation and "to express public policy in the distribution of wealth and income, as in the case of the progressive income and estate taxes."

Not many said it too loudly, but everyone came to recognize it. "Pay as you go" was the fiscal equivalent of the war's wonder weapons. It was a wonder weapon that would be deployed in peacetime, and that would change the way Americans felt about their government forever.

The Grandest Sticker Shock

Most Americans come face-to-face with Beardsley Ruml and his pipe at the moment that they get their first paycheck. First they look at the bottom number, rather less than they thought it was going to be. Then, and only then, do they start to puzzle over the items. "Gross," "income tax," "disability," "state," "F.I.C.A." Then, again, they look to the disappointing bit Mr. Ruml has left them. The name they give that amount reflects the fresh cynicism of people beginning to understand the way life works: "take-home."

That first-paycheck moment—call it the grandest of all life's sticker shocks—is something many Americans recall well. In fact most of us remember the sight of that check in our hands in much the same way we remember the dashboard of our first car. So this is adulthood, we said to ourselves. We like the car memory. We don't like the withholding memory, so we try to ignore it. Why remind ourselves of something that we cannot change? It is hard to imagine saving the amount we pay in tax each year, and then sending the money in one giant check come April 15. Confronted with the idea of sending $10,000 or $20,000 to the government all at once, some of us would surely revolt. But taxpayers no longer have a chance to do even that. The Internal Revenue Service calls our tax system "voluntary," but the IRS doesn't ask. It just takes.

This book seeks to capture the American experience with our tax structure, the strange and powerful machine Beardsley Ruml set in motion. Withholding does not describe the whole of our tax lives. Indeed, many of our taxes—sales taxes, property taxes—are not even collected through withholding. But in the half century since Ruml acted, withholding has become a valuable symbol of our tax experience, an experience we have come to question. Today, voters consistently name the income tax when asked what things they would like to see politicians change. They also name Social Security, another form of tax. And, very often, they name schools and property taxes, yet a third problem with an enormous tax component. Indeed, a *Washington Post*/ABC poll published in the summer of 1998 showed that education, Social Security, and overhauling the tax system—all three items matters of tax—were more on voters' minds than anything else.

When we stop to consider, this is not surprising. Today, taxes touch, edit, even limit our lives at every stage. Taxes tie down young workers from their very first day on the job. The rate of payroll taxes confronting an eighteen-year-old starting out at McDonald's today—7.65 percent—is higher than the income tax rate Congress reserved for millionaires—7 percent—in 1913, the year the income tax was born. Sales taxes punish our purchases. Property taxes rise, yet we find ourselves more and more dissatisfied with our schools. Income taxes pull down families: married couples pay more than two single earners with the same combined income. Married women who want to work pay a special surcharge to Uncle Sam for doing so, the so-called marriage penalty. Taxes punish midcareer Americans at the moment they are straining hardest to achieve—indeed, at the moment of their first successes. Professionals find themselves moving from cities—to avoid New York's unincorporated business tax, for example—or becoming avid conservationists to obtain one of the greatest modern tax bonuses, a formerly obscure advantage known as the conservation easement. Complicated tax rules often cast senior citizens in their sixties into a sort of purgatory, a purgatory where they have to be careful not to "earn too much." Sometimes, taxes even turn senior citizens into refugees—we euphemistically call them "snow birds"—who depart their homes rather than confront tax bills.

A world ordinarily as away from tax as one can get—the world of sports—saw an example of this in the summer of 1998. In the beginning of September, it became clear that Mark McGwire of the St. Louis Cardinals stood a good chance of breaking Roger Maris's season record of 61 home runs. When McGwire tied that record, speculators began calculating the worth of the historic sixty-second ball, which some sports experts put at $1 million. Before the game, the consensus in this, the best-hearted of sports, became clear: any fan who caught the million-dollar prize ought to nonetheless give it to McGwire, the man who earned it.

In stepped the tax experts. It emerged that receiving, and then giving, such a ball might mean that the bleacher fan would be subject to a $145,000 odd bill for "gift taxes." In the mini-firestorm of outrage that ensued, Congress moved to pass a special dispensation for the lucky fielder, and the IRS backed off. It issued a statement assuring that it would not dun any fan who instantly gave the ball back to McGwire. And indeed, the stadium staffer who retrieved the ball instantly returned it, telling reporters: "I just don't want to be taxed." A bright moment of summer serendipity dimmed as fans across the nation pondered this heretofore unimaginable thing: a tax on joy.

People are marvelously adaptable. Forced as we are to

live in a world of tax, we have found ways to ensure that not all our tax experiences are unpleasant. Under the conservation easement arrangement, for example, wealthy property owners trade some of the rights to their property—principally the right to build new structures on that space—for a good-sized tax break. In this exchange, they are winners, for most of them never intended to develop their tranquil summer refuges anyway. Indeed, the fact that their property remains pristine actually adds to its value on the real estate market. At the middle of the income scale, taxpayers take a kind of vengeful joy in the credits that the tax man makes available to them. In 1998, 48 million taxpayers leveled their income tax bills—but not their social security bill—all the way down to zero by using such breaks.

Still, there is a sense this is a loser's game. It is not that Americans don't want to pay taxes; they do. It is that they feel that taxes have moved out of proportion to what is fair, or appropriate. Even if we approve of certain government-spending projects, we sense that the whole affair has moved out of control. We all say we want a smaller government, yet each year Americans are compelled to hand over to our treasury $1.48 trillion, or a sum of money equal to the size of the economy of Great Britain. Nobody who is working today signed on for this.

Long ago, the philosophers who inspired our country's founding and early years anticipated this dilemma. They laid out powerful images that depict the forces affecting our pocketbooks to this day. Adam Smith described the "invisible hand," the hand of free commerce that brings magic order and harmony to our lives. Thomas Paine wrote of another hand, all too visible and intrusive: "the greedy hand of government, thrusting itself into every corner and crevice of industry." Today the invisible hand is a very busy one. Markets are wider and freer than ever, and we profit from that by living better than before. But the "greedy hand of government" is also at work. Indeed, in relative terms, the greedy hand has grown faster than the invisible hand. In the late 1990s, economists noted with astonishment that federal taxes made up one-fifth of the economy, a rate higher than at any time in American history outside of war. We can not assign the blame for changes of such magnitude to Beardsley Ruml, who was, after all, not much more than a New Deal package man. The real force here is not even withholding, whatever its power. Behind Ruml's withholding lurks Paine's greedy hand.

The modern thinker who dedicated himself to the study of the greedy hand's expansion is the Nobel Prize winner James Buchanan, the father of a school of economics called public choice theory. Public choice theory says that government is like any other industry: it wants to survive, and it wants to compete. Like a business in the market, it will work hard to damage challengers, even other parts of government. Government offices compete with private businesses. The IRS competes with individuals for their livelihood. Government grows reflexively, often in spite of the best efforts of reform-minded government officials. When it happens upon a tool like withholding, and marshals that tool in its service, it begins to grow very fast. The shift frightens people—it is what leads them to refer to *Government,* with a capital *G.* It is what transforms a reasonable public sector in a reasonable society—ours—into Paine's flamboyant greedy hand.

There are several things Americans know about the way the greedy hand works today. One is that the greedy hand is, indeed, greedy. Every year the Tax Foundation, a Washington-based think tank, does math that confirms the impression of a growing burden. The Foundation starts by calculating the "Tax Freedom Day" for that year. It adds up the total tax burden on Americans, federal, state, and local, and then tabulates the number of days that the average American must work to pay all those taxes. In 1902, the average American had to work to January 31 before his annual tax obligation, something like one-twelfth of his income, was met. By 1940, the date was March 8. In 1974, or a year when the nation was feeling the full pain of bracket creep, Tax Freedom Day was May 2. In 1997, it was May 9. In 1998, it was May 10, the latest day in history. Americans must work more than a third of their year before Paine's apparition stops taking and they begin to keep what they earn. The Tax Foundation found another troubling fact: each year Tax Freedom Day is set to move up the calendar—as long as we keep the current system.

Then there is another problem: the degree to which taxes intrude on the average American family. The Tax Foundation's charts show that in 1957, a family with two earners paid something like a quarter of their budget in taxes—well under the amount the family spent for food and housing. In 1998, that same two-earner family gave back nearly 40 percent to local, state, and federal authorities in taxes. That means the family pays more in taxes than it spends for food, clothing, and housing combined.

Often, we are not aware of the full extent of the tax take. The average cost of a restaurant meal today is $40. Eleven of those dollars go directly to taxes. Twenty-nine dollars go to making the meal and serving it. Americans for Tax Reform, a conservative Washington tax group, compiled a list of all the taxes that make up that $11. That list was longer than many a menu. There were federal income taxes, federal payroll taxes, state income taxes, state sales taxes, and state use taxes. There were unemployment insurance taxes, workers' comp taxes, state property taxes, business license taxes, local property and income taxes, telephone taxes, utility taxes, and liquor taxes.

Indeed, the burden is even bigger than the better-known numbers suggest. In 1997, Americans spent just a tad over 20 percent of the gross domestic product on federal taxes, indeed the highest level since the United States was striking back at the Japanese and Hitler. Widen that to include all the other levies we pay and the figure rises to 30 percent of the gross domestic product, another peacetime record.

So the greedy hand takes more than before. But, as important, it also takes in a different way than it used to. The American tax system has changed, changed while most Americans were not looking. In the 1960s, for example, the tax treatment of business was a principal preoccupation. So too were the high marginal tax rates on individuals and the outlandish tax deductions available to them. The word loophole was associated with top earners. As recently as 1990, one economics textbook instructed students that complications like tax loopholes were largely upper-crust affairs: "because of our progressive tax system, many tax loopholes are beneficial only to taxpayers in higher income tax brackets."

Taxes still slow businesses' growth today. Shareholders, a

group that now includes many tens of millions of citizens, lose out because of double and triple taxation on their stock. Income taxes still punish the very wealthy, although not at quite the same rates as before. Indexing the bracket in our tax schedule to inflation has stopped many of the hidden tax increases that were the rule in the 1970s and 1980s. The 1986 tax reform pruned back many of the older, more picturesque deductions—tales of incorporated yachts and three-martini lunches come to mind.

These days, though, the middle class is the one mired in tax troubles. Social Security, once a marginal levy, is now a giant one. If you count our employers' share of our Social Security tax, as most economists do, the burden looks particularly heavy: Social Security is the greatest tax for a full 70 percent of Americans. If private school enrollment is any measure, our schools, one of the more important tax purchases, disappoint us more now than ever before. Income taxes also punish us in a new way. We no longer have the inflationary bracket creep that punished us in the 1970s. But we have what economists call "real bracket creep"—as we earn more, we move into tax brackets we never expected would apply to us. Even the lofty loophole has become a middle-class project. One of the Book-of-the-Month Club choices in 1998 was even titled *101 Tax Loopholes for the Middle Class.* The jacket copy stressed carefully that the book was "geared specifically to MIDDLE INCOME taxpayers." And these loopholes often prove to be snares, particularly for the harder workers among us.

The third thing we dislike about taxes is that they are unpredictable. Today our tax code is so large that no one, certainly not the civil servants at the IRS, can consistently apply it. The internal revenue code has a total of 1.3 million words, or over twice the length of *War and Peace.* The tax-code regulations that are the sibling to the code number 5.75 million words, or just about eight times as many as the Bible. Citizens doubt, legitimately, that such a voluminous body of law can be consistently applied.

For the wealthiest of Americans, people long accustomed to complicated rules, this costly and time-consuming paperwork may not matter so much. They have their tax attorneys and their accountants, with whom they may work in sometimes cynical symbiosis: "It's a game," as one attorney in the Paramount film of John Grisham's *The Firm* told another. "We teach the rich how to play it so they can stay rich—and the IRS keeps changing the rules so we can keep getting rich teaching them." Even the wealthiest have lost track of why the taxes are being exacted.

For most citizens, though, the complexity is unnerving. Americans make their best effort to pay their tax bills. For many years, they were so good about it that American public finance was the envy of European and Asian tax collectors. But the system has become so complex that it is hard to tell if we are doing the right thing, no matter how industriously we try. Will Rogers, a humorist who regaled the nation earlier in the century, put it this way: when we Americans fill out a tax return, we don't know whether we are a crook or a martyr.

This uncertainty damages our lives in a subtle way. It makes honest people live in fear that the government may one day tell them they are something that they never intended to be—scofflaws, cheats. This is why so many Americans follow hearings featuring IRS horror stories with fascination. It is why ordinarily sedate citizens are moved to empathize with tax protestors or even outright tax-evading kooks.

In the 1960s, IRS audit rates were relatively high. In 1968, for example, the IRS announced that one in twenty-five taxpayers could expect to be questioned on exemptions they had claimed, their charitable deductions or medical costs. Today the IRS conducts audits at half that rate. Yet more Americans, particularly lower earners, know they have legitimate reason to fear they *might* be audited. Their fear magnifies the might of the IRS.

Indeed, there is concrete evidence of how Americans fear the tax man. In 1997, individuals across the country paid about $100 billion more in taxes than they needed to. That meant they forsook several billion in interest their money could have earned had they kept it—the price of security. Self-employed citizens who are not subject to withholding and must calculate their own tax bills quarterly are particularly frightened. Indeed many complain that they would rather have the security of withholding than the fear of being audited that comes with their freedom. The game has turned so treacherous that the withholding cage has come to feel like a safe place. At some firms, employees even ask management to begin withholding. In other words, in America today, people beg to be taxed.

This is a modern version of a phenomenon Adam Smith described precisely in his *Wealth of Nations*. When there are no fixed rules, the philosopher wrote, we are all "more or less in the power of the tax gatherer." In a society with a tax code like ours, a code even accountants cannot decipher, people are no longer sure that they are safe on theirs, the legal side of the society's great divide. The moment you sense that you yourself may one day have to do battle with authorities is the moment you find yourself beginning to empathize with the fugitive.

Still, there is something else troubling Americans. The issue is not merely the scale of the taxes, however extraordinary that scale. It is not merely the changes, however unintended their result. It is not merely the unpredictability, although that unpredictability is infuriating. There is a specific cause for this new detachment and anger. It is that, in modern America, the greedy hand isn't merely greedy, or different than before, or unpredictable. It is also meddling, bossy, intrusive. Today our tax code doesn't stop at merely taking its share. It also wants to tell people how to live.

This last change has been, in large part, intentional. In this half-century, the era of our modern tax life, lawmakers have not contented themselves with writing tax laws with the aim of capturing revenue. They have indeed absorbed New Deal–era lessons and used Ruml's tool to try to change behavior and lives. And in recent decades, as welfare has fallen from favor, their tax-meddling habit has become stronger. Republicans and Democrats agreed that social engineering through entitlements wasn't yielding the results they sought. So they began pouring all their energy, energy that used to go into constructing welfare projects, into the tax code. The fussier and more specific the project, the more attractive it seems. The tobacco tax legislation of 1998, legislation that did not, in the end, become law, is a classic example. Lawmakers sought to use taxes to punish one group—smokers—so they could reward another group: married couples. The Earned Income Credit is another example. This tiny program, a tax rebate designed to hearten low-income workers and keep them from dropping out of the workforce, has morphed into a $30 billion project that shapes millions of Americans' lives.

Such projects are well intended. But it is important to stop to consider how the taxpayer views them. In Ruml's days, the exigencies of the war made us want to give to the government. Even after the war—in the Eisenhower administration, say—well over half of tax revenues were going to outlays the average citizens understood and approved of: building a military capable of facing down the Russians, laying the interstate highway system. The national tax commitment stretched into the 1960s, when voters felt that their tax money might work to justify great social wrongs—urban poverty, or racism.

A 1953 episode of Jackie Gleason's *The Honeymooners* dramatizes the commitment to taxes Americans once felt. Ralph Kramden, the down-at-the-heels bus driver, is at first angry at discovering he owes the government $15 in extra taxes—he had saved that money toward a new bowling ball. But when he considers the matter, he decides he is glad to pay the tax. "We're living in a great country," he tells Alice, in a display of lachrymose remorse one is hard put to imagine finding in our modern post-*Seinfeld* sitcoms. "I didn't mean that before what I said about the income tax. Boy, we should give everything to the government. Especially this government."

Today though, very few Americans feel the sort of connection that Ralph spoke of. And little wonder—the cold war has ended, and they have become skeptical of the efficiency of Great Society outlays. Today, more than half of the budget goes to social transfers mandated by expensive programs whose value many Americans question. Working citizens sense that someone is getting something, but that someone is often not they.

The avid tax haters who pop up occasionally in the news are the expression of this national unease. Their froth-mouthed manifestos strike us as extreme—how many of us truly want to "kill the IRS"?—but they reflect something that all Americans feel to some degree. Even the most moderate of us often feel a tick of sympathy when we hear the shouts of the tax haters. We think of our forefathers who felt compelled to rebel against the Crown for "imposing Taxes on us without our consent." We know we live in a democracy, and so must have chosen this arrangement. Yet nowadays we too find ourselves feeling that taxes are imposed on us "without our consent."

Washington doesn't necessarily recognize the totality of this tax frustration. The purview of the House Ways and Means Committee is limited to federal taxes, and so the committee writes tax law as if the federal income tax were the only tax in the country. The commissions that monitor Social Security concern themselves only with the solvency of Social Security, and so ignore the consequences of raising payroll taxes, or taxing pensions, at a time when income taxes are already high. Old programs with outdated aims stay in place. Newer ones, added piecemeal, often conflict with the old.

"Rube Goldberg machine," "unstoppable contraption"— none of the stock phrases adequately captures the complication that is our tax structure. As William E. Simon, a former Treasury secretary, once said, "The nation should have a tax system which looks like someone designed it on purpose."

A good share of the blame for the current situation lies

with the nation's powerful lobbies, which often operate in a predatory mode that seems to confirm their reptilian reputation. Each of many dozens of tax loopholes in our code—tax "expenditures" in budget language—has its own representation office on Washington's Dupont Circle, or in Virginia. Their colorful battles have preoccupied journalists who covered Washington for the past twenty years. Today Washington boasts some 80,000 lobbyists, double the number from the mid-1970s. Senator Tim Hutchinson's staff calculated that with each 10,000 additional lobbyists, we have added 100,000 new words to the tax code.

Over the years, there have been various efforts to right this situation. There have been attacks on withholding. After war's end—after the emergency that was supposed to justify it ended with peace—withholding again faced its challenges. Some of those came from regular citizens, who were shocked that the process continued after the war. In the late 1940s, a Connecticut cable-grip maker named Vivien Kellems actually tried to create a movement to protest the withholding. She refused to withhold for the hundred-odd employees of her company, and challenged the IRS collectors in federal court. She even wrote a fiery volume of protest titled *Toil, Taxes and Trouble.*

"Under the hypnosis of war hysteria, with a pusillanimous Congress rubber-stamping every whim of the White House, we passed the withholding tax. We appointed ourselves so many policemen and with this club in our hands, we set out to collect a tax from every hapless individual who received wages from us." Kellems supporters packed tea bags, their emblems of tax protest, into envelopes to send to Wilbur Mills, then the powerful chairman of the House

Ways and Means. Her protest even earned her respect in serious quarters: Harry Reasoner compared her battle to that of Gandhi and Martin Luther King. Most people, though, depicted her as a kook: Kellems spent her waning years holding forth at the soirées of the far-right fringe.

The Adolph Coors family also tried to protest. The papers reported Coors wanted to show workers the scope of the government take. It gave them their full pay—without withholding—for two months. In the third month it took out three months' worth of withholding. Yet soon Coors abandoned its no-withholding experiment. Years later Coors's executives recall the event as an artifact from ancient history.

In recent decades, at different points, politicians have also tried to challenge withholding. Ronald Reagan talked about challenging state withholding in his campaign for California governor—but did not follow through while in office. In the mid-1990s, House majority leader Dick Armey pushed through a plan to end withholding with his flat-tax proposal. Instead of the annual 1040 reconciliation, Americans would make monthly payments in their tax bill—"rather like a monthly car payment."

Alarmed at Americans' anger and goaded by IRS horror stories, Congress in 1998 raced to pass an IRS reform law. But the 1998 IRS reform, like other IRS reforms that preceded it, merely addressed the symptoms. In the summer of 1998, after the law's passage, taxpayers were still naming an overhaul of the tax code as a change they heartily desired.

From time to time our leaders have even launched attacks on the tax beast itself. In the 1960s, the Kennedy administration led a historic and successful effort to pull down rates. In the 1980s and 1990s our federal deficit— a deficit that resulted from government's commitment to projects many voters questioned—stalled tax-cutting plans. Nonetheless Ronald Reagan and a Democratic Congress pulled together the powerful tax reform of 1986, a reform which did much to fuel the growth that we have seen since that point.

But politicians, however hard they have tried to right things, must be called to account. The Democrats' damage has come mostly as a result of their cloth-earned focus on equity. Americans move with incredible alacrity up and down the social ladder. Many families rise from poverty to the middle class in one lifetime; and many travel in the opposite direction. Democrats have generally ignored this, treating citizens as if they were locked into their social classes like so many characters in *Upstairs, Downstairs*, the British soap opera about an Edwardian household. The result has been laws that often punish people for making it into the parlor and even remove them, from time to time, to the scullery.

Conservatives have done their share of the dirty work. Republicans led the way in replacing the welfare state with the tax code as government's principal social engineering tool. Sometimes, as in Friedman's withholding story, the results of their work were unintentional. At other times the conservatives planned their damage. President Bush and his colleagues knew what they were doing—although they didn't, perhaps, think it through—when in 1990 they led the move to undo the only solid tax reform in recent years, the 1986 Act. In a panic over the budget and the Gulf War,

Bush reversed his campaign pledge of "Read my lips: no new taxes" and raised income tax rates. This soured voters on politicians' talk of tax reform—if betrayal came so easily, why trust new promises? As important, the switch so disillusioned many of the leaders who had pushed for 1980s changes that they are hesitant to step forward to lead tax reform now.

Lately both parties find themselves mired in a new and vicious cycle. The cycle starts with taxpayers, who cry out to lawmakers for tax relief. The politicians are eager to respond. The Republican party was so eager in 1994 that it made taxes one of the planks of its Contract with America, and made abolishing the marriage penalty its priority in 1998.

But rather than adopt wholescale reform, the lawmakers try to give relief through tiny, symbolic projects. The family child credit of the Contract with America was one such project. The White House and Democratic lawmakers focus on helping the family by expanding the Earned Income Credit, a cash rebate for low earners. They cobble together new versions of IRAs, or obsess about improving day-care credits.

In the short term, voters seem to like these devices. The idea of tax relief plays well in focus groups, a fact all-important to our anxious politicians. Little tax breaks even win elections. Only later, after the election, after these little efforts take effect, do voters discover the puny size of a break, or the hidden perversities that attend it. Then they turn angry. Indeed, their anger about tax is one reason they check out of the political process. This sets the politicians rambling about "political disillusionment." And it panics them into yet another round of engineering. The president speaks of targeted tax breaks; lawmakers plan further fiddles. Voters turn away. Our tax weariness is an important counterpart to our general political disillusionment, the sort of weariness the writer E. J. Dionne sought to convey in his thoughtful book, *Why Americans Hate Politics.*

There is a way out of this confusion. It is to drop the pursuit of solutions for a moment, a moment in which we actually consider the problem. It is to review how the whole apparatus functions, how it pervades, dampens, and makes knots of our lives. It is to go back and take a deeper look at the underlying assumptions of the tax writers—that taxing "the rich" is the best way to bring us all justice, that tiny targeted breaks are the best way to help families—to see whether they really make sense in the context of a freer and more fluid society. It is to understand how we have all, even the politicians, become servants of this improbable regime. The first step to shutting out the greedy hand is to unveil it at work.

2

YOUR CLOTHES

WHAT'S THE BIGGEST TOURIST DESTINATION IN AMERICA? Disney World and the Epcot Center, in Florida? The Grand Canyon? Graceland, perhaps?

The answer is none of the above. The nation's proudest leisure-time travel destination is a seven-year-old collection of square footage in a second-ring suburb of Minneapolis–St. Paul. It is the Mall of America, a megamall so huge its developers once referred to it as the Ninth Wonder of the World. Visitors come from neighboring states like North Dakota and Iowa. They also come, and in great number, from Illinois, New York, and California. They even fly in from Winnipeg, Amsterdam, London, and Osaka. Every year the Mall of America gets nine times as many visitors as the entire population of Minnesota. Its traffic of 42 million a year makes the Mall of America a larger attraction than the Big Three of tourism combined.

In some ways, the Mall of America is any mall. It has Macy's. It has B. Dalton. It has Sears. It has a teenager problem, at times so bad that one year it had to institute a special policy of "escorted kids only." Like most modern malls, it cocoons shoppers from the harsher elements. Its air temperature is "seventy degrees, all the time," an advantage not to be dismissed in an iceland like Minnesota in February.

But the Mall of America also has things no other American mall can compete with. It has more stores than any other American mall, 520 of them. It has an amusement park called Knott's Camp Snoopy, where parents can park their children to play on a million dollars' worth of equipment, including a roller coaster. It has UnderWater World, a 1.2-million-gallon walk-through aquarium that takes visitors on a simulated trip of the nation's waterways. It has Golf Mountain, an eighteen-hole miniature-golf course. It has novelties like the Rainforest Cafe, where real mist sprays into the air over lunchers and thunderstorms—complete with lightning—happen every twenty minutes. And it has one other, powerful attraction: the Mall of America is a tax haven. Minnesota charges no sales tax on clothing.

At Play with the Greedy Hand

Tax shopping is a national pastime in this country, a game Americans take up frequently and sometimes seriously. Economists have all kinds of labels for this behavior—they call it things like "tax arbitrage" and build charts around it. In reality tax shopping depicts something simpler: citizens at play with the greedy hand. Governments, in this case state and local authorities, try to pretend the hand isn't there and that it isn't greedy—what's a 6 percent levy here, a little 1 percent charge there? People for their part don't fight with government head on: you rarely see a crowd picketing against a sales tax. But they do dodge and duck, dancing away from the greedy hand to shop where it can't reach. And their faces do show a trace of satisfaction: "I'm here to get something, and I'm getting it now. This is my turn."

These days, this play often seems lighthearted. Americans don't evade sales taxes on anything like the scale Europeans do. There a punitive sales tax called the value-added tax, a tax with rates of 15 percent, 17 percent, 18 percent, and more, has converted the tax fun to an out-and-out war. A black market in everything from autos to plumbing services thrives on the Continent. But there are plenty of signs, signs that show up in their tax shopping, that Americans too are ready to break the law—to have real fun—the moment they decide that Paine's hand is intruding too far. It was not for nothing that the Boston Tea Party was called a *party.*

The national game starts with the states, towns, and counties, the levels of government that control most sales taxes. These governments set their tax rates—often rates that differ from one another's. And shoppers respond—by surveying their options and buying at the best price—the price with the lowest tax. Every day purchasing decisions are made on the basis of tax shopping. Americans look for low taxes for the same reasons they wait for sales or transport themselves to outlet malls in rural backlands or buy products that come with cash rebates. They want to save a few pennies. Saving a few pennies along the way makes them feel a little better about the decision to shop that they made in the first place. Not all the tax shopping in this country involves such extravagant excursions as a pilgrimage to the Mall of America. From Florida to Alaska, American citizens regularly cross town, county, and state borders in the name of saving on taxes when we shop.

How important are these decisions? Taxes are rarely the main reason Americans name for choosing to shop the way they do. But they are always *a* factor, a factor that places like the Mall of America have proven can be worth hundreds of millions of dollars. Indeed, tax shopping has grown so much in recent years that businesses that didn't have a tax advantage—in this instance, retailers in high-tax states—felt the need to send an ambassador to Washington to warn the House Committee on Small Business that the tax-free world was growing so fast it soon might kill off that most American thing, the old-fashioned, full-tax retail mall.

Among consumers, the American tax-shopping game has distinct winners and losers. Take the examples of Washington State and Oregon: Washington has no income tax, and Oregon has no sales tax. Citizens of Washington's border towns, therefore, drive over the Columbia River to Portland, Oregon, to do their shopping, avoiding both levies. They have their tax cake and eat it too. The losers in that equation are Oregonians. The reverse trip up Interstate 5 gains them nothing, except the opportunity to pay Washington sales tax along with their home income tax. In Illinois and other old, industrial states, the losers are city dwellers—cities like Chicago and New York tend to charge urban shoppers an extra penny or more in sales tax on their consumption. In Louisiana the losers are Louisianans: the state offers a rebate on sales taxes to foreign visitors, but locals must pay the full levy. In Florida the losers are people with weak bladders. Gas taxes change from county to county, and the fixed-income crowd tend to pick their rest stops accordingly.

Part of the challenge confronting the players of the tax

game is that the tax-scape doesn't stay the same. From time to time lawmakers will change the rules—often, it seems, just to amuse themselves. But the pleasure of victory for tax shoppers is important to them, so important that they willingly fight back by traveling farther, or altering their habits yet again, just to keep their tax breaks.

The Mall's Story

To see the full extent of the shopping-tax game, it helps to look at a place like the Mall of America. For starters, it is no accident that the mall, which could be sited anywhere, chose Bloomington for its site. When they were ready to build, the mall's developers did some tax shopping of their own. They obtained various tax favors to undertake the project, a daring one given its scope and the fact that, at the time, America lay mired in a recession. The mall got tax breaks on $100 million in financing from Bloomington to help it build its parking decks and transit station where public buses arrive.

Minnesotans themselves don't gain any advantage on clothing tax by driving to Bloomington—they don't pay tax on clothing anywhere in the state. But if they choose to eat at the Mall of America, they get a break. That's because the Mall of America doesn't have a restaurant tax, whereas the Twin Cities, for example, have a 3.5 percent levy. Minnesotans' overall tax load is high: when the Tax Foundation, a Washington think tank that charts tax burdens, compared Minnesotans' total tax load with that of citizens of other states, it found that Minnesotans' burden was among the heaviest in the nation—only tax hells like New York or

California were worse. So some citizens of Minneapolis–
St. Paul notice that they are saving when they choose to
show relatives a good time at the Rainforest Cafe.

When it comes to out-of-state shoppers, the tax game at
the Mall of America gets serious. Wisconsin, Iowa, North
Dakota, and South Dakota all have a 5 percent tax on clothing. The fact that Minnesota has none is an accident of the
state's progressive Northern European heritage. State lawmakers long held that taxing necessities like clothing and
food put an unjust burden on the poor. Today Minnesota's
progressivism is fading, but the progressives' work is still in
place. Clothing—all clothing—is tax-free. You have to wonder whether the state's fathers, doubtless stuffy fellows all,
actually envisioned young women converging from four
states to slither into tax-free camisoles in the dressing rooms
of the mall's two Victoria's Secret shops. But that's what
happens.

Indeed, Minnesota's clothing-tax advantage helps ensure
that the Mall of America is a regional shoppers' mecca.
When time comes for a spree, many of them hop into one of
the shuttle flights Northwest Airlines operates to Minnesota
and the Mall of America. Northwest WorldVacations, the
tour operator for Northwest Airlines, saw a 47 percent increase in package passengers to the Mall of America from
North American cities in the first quarter of 1998 over 1997.

Miles as Money

The savviest of the tax shoppers don't pay for such flights.
They use another tax advantage—their "miles"—to get to
Minnesota. Frequent-flier miles are a marketing phenome-

non, a trick airlines and now credit card companies have learned to use to build customer loyalty. But, in their way, miles are also a form of tax shopping. Many people build up their miles while working. When their employers let them keep the miles, they are giving the employees something of value—income that neither employer nor employee pays tax on. In this sense, miles really are tax-free money, which escapes the greedy hand altogether.

Then there are the international tax gamesters, more than two million of them a year by the mall's count. Citizens of Winnipeg pay Canada's onerous goods and services tax, which is 7 percent. Manitoba drops an additional 7 percent on top of that. With Northwest offering flights from Winnipeg at $258 round trip, the draw of saving 14 percent begins to look worthwhile. Shoppers know that if they stay forty-eight hours, Canadian customs will allow them to bring up to $500 in purchases back home, duty-free. (The deal is $200 in purchases for shorter stays.) Are tax savings important to these shoppers? "Big factor," sums up one of Northwest's booking agents telegraphically.

Among these arrivals number the *truly* international tax shoppers. Europeans and Asians pay giant sales taxes ranging in the high teens. The evidence: Minnesota's Minneapolis–St. Paul International Airport has 240 international flights a week—seven each from Tokyo, Osaka, and London, and twenty-one from Amsterdam. This is up from a mere sixty-one in the mall's younger days. Frankfurt added on a direct flight for summer shopping. "Jerusalem has the Wall, but Minneapolis has the Mall," announced the Jerusalem *Post* from high-tax Israel. In August 1997 the Minneapolis *Star Tribune* reported what has to be the ultimate tax-travel factoid: couples from ten countries have held their weddings in the Mall of America's little chapel.

Some of this international behavior is due to another kind of economic pastime: currency shopping. The dollar in this decade has been relatively weak, so that foreigners from developed countries can buy more with their money here than they can at home. But a good part of it is taxes. You can tell this because foreigners often betray an expertise worthy of a state revenue official when it comes to the minutiae of our sales-tax laws. Switzerland's stuffy *Neue Zuercher Zeitung* complained that not everything in America was a bargain—"especially when you're looking for the sort of quality the Swiss are accustomed to." The paper's reporter, though, went on to hand his readership a few well-valued tax tips: "In the city of Chicago, 8.75 percent is the rule, but in the bordering parts of Illinois, it's only 6 percent. In New York a sweater from the same retail chain costs 2.25 percent more than in Florida. For foreigners New Orleans is particularly attractive. There you can get sales tax that you've paid back at the border." The title of the article? "America, Land of Unlimited Shopping."

All this activity has made a deep impression on Minnesota's tourism officials, who for years had only more traditional attractions like the state's fifteen thousand–odd blue lakes, or the Edward Hopper at Minneapolis's Walker Art Center to compete with. The mall elevated Minnesota to a new class as a tourist destination, and the officials know that tax is part of that. The government employees are of course not eager to spell out the amounts of business they are taking away from fellow states and foreign governments. But they do confirm that tax is a huge component of their tourism success. "I can't say it's fifty percent, but it's a big share," says Brian Dietz of Minnesota's Department of Trade and Economic Development.

Indeed, when Minnesota had good news about taxes to give its citizens, the Mall of America was one of the places it chose to make its announcement. On one Friday in February of 1998, Minnesotans who shopped at the Mall of America encountered a new entity: a huge felt frog figure, the "Tax Frog," who handed out tax forms that would allow them to collect a statewide tax rebate. The state's revenue officials sent out a wire explaining helpfully why they had chosen a frog as their symbol. "The answer is simply because frogs say, 'rebate-rebate.' "

IKEA's Example

The Mall of America is only the most visible symbol of this kind of activity. New York City, for example, clearly has it over Bloomington when it comes to the variety of attractions it offers. But when it comes to shopping, New York citizens spurn their hometown. They have a single word they use to describe their tax shopping—"IKEA." IKEA, pronounced "i-KEE-a," is a Swedish housewares giant. The store closest to New Yorkers is located in a place highly inconvenient to them: an old industrial park off the highway in Elizabeth, New Jersey. But New Yorkers travel to IKEA quite willingly—by car through the clogged Holland Tunnel or by special, free IKEA buses departing the city's grimy Port Authority terminal on the half hour.

IKEA, like Mall of America, has many attractions. It is giant—shoppers confront thousands of articles, all displayed in a charming, Swedish manner. But its most powerful attraction is, arguably, its tax rate. Elizabeth, New Jersey, is an urban enterprise zone with a sales-tax rate all its own: 3 percent. Since New Yorkers normally pay 8.25 percent, they save over $5 per hundred dollars. So many of them apparently found this deal worth it that New York's department of revenue got excited. In IKEA's early days, they sent revenue officials to IKEA's parking lot to note down New York shoppers' license plate numbers so they could go after them by claiming a "use tax" on goods imported to New York. This caused a lot of disgruntlement among shoppers.

New York shoppers in search of clothing and shoes also travel outside their state to evade an 8.25 percent sales tax. The numbers crunchers estimate that the state's retailers lose something like $700 million in sales just because people choose to buy clothes outside of New York rather than pay the tax. Pennsylvania newspapers brag that the state's booming outlet business—no sales tax on clothes or shoes—has made it the "outlet capital of the world."

Indiana has enjoyed a similar advantage for cigarettes. In May 1994 neighboring Michigan raised its cigarette tax from 25¢ to 75¢ a pack, the second-highest in the nation, according to scholar Patrick Fleenor and Price Waterhouse, who made a study of it. During the next year, Fleenor reports, cigarette sales fell in Michigan by 26.7 percent. Just across the border, though, many Indiana store owners found cigarette sales rising up to 40 percent. The reason was clear: consumers who drove from Union Pier, Michigan—to name a border town—down the road to Michigan City, Indiana, saved $5.95 in taxes on each carton they bought.

There are those too who respond to tax intrusions in the opposite way: by *not* shopping, or by shopping at a moment when the greedy hand isn't around. The state of Alaska found this out the hard way when it planned a huge increase in its cigarette tax, to a dollar a pack. The tax was to go into effect October 1, 1997. Smokers struck back by buying an astounding 175 million more cigarettes than usual in the three months before the tax deadline. Richard Watts of the Great Alaska Tobacco Company told the local papers that some smokers even bought sixty-carton cases—at $1,200 each—rather than pay the tax. As for Alaska's Department of Revenue, it saw its revenue estimates go up in smoke: collections slowed 60 percent following the infamous increase date.

L. L. Bean

Most tax shoppers know yet another way to play the game with the greedy hand: by mail. When a Californian or a Pennsylvanian orders from L. L. Bean in Maine, California's and Pennsylvania's revenue departments would dearly like to collect tax on that purchase. But states don't have power over interstate commerce—Congress does— and Congress can't—and won't—enforce a state tax. So local tax authorities from California (6 percent base rate), Illinois (base rate 6.25 percent), Nevada (6.5 percent), and Pennsylvania (6 percent) lose when their citizens shop by mail at L. L. Bean. So, by the way, do the local tax authorities in those states: Maine may be home to L. L. Bean, but its authorities don't get the sales tax either. In many cases money saved in tax on a pair of sweaters just about offsets the price of the shipping bill, a pleasure that does not elude shoppers. Everyone likes the feeling of getting a UPS package for "free."

Frustrated states of course do their best to pursue the escaping revenue, which one group estimated at $3 billion a year. But this is an area where consumer rage commands some respect. When the Direct Marketing Association, the lobby that represents the mail-order giants, opened negotiations with the various states to work toward a general collection arrangement, shoppers protested. The mail-order houses saw the light. Suddenly, everyone was denying plans to collect the sales taxes. On fax letterhead complete with leaping stag and trout, L. L. Bean responded to an inquiry from *The Wall Street Journal* on the matter that the firm "has no plans to change its practices . . . related to sales tax collection for out-of-state orders."

The high end of the market is also adroit in tax shopping. Over the years, European car makers have offered a tempting package to American customers. They invite car buyers to make their purchases in Europe, sometimes lacing the packages with free plane tickets and dinners in castles. The price tag for such BMWs and Saabs is an attractive one, sometimes as much as 10 percent less than the American sticker price. "Fly to Sweden on us and come home with quite a souvenir," ran a Saab ad campaign. And, as *The New York Times* tells the story, customers who travel abroad to pick up their vehicles sometimes sweeten the arrangement by using it to elude the taxman. They return their autos to the states, but don't report their European purchases to authorities, thereby avoiding a 7 percent federal luxury tax as well as various state levies. Recently the

IRS, though, picked up on the action and began leaning on car makers and buyers, spoiling much of the fun.

A Serious Conversation

At some point the question intrudes: what's going on? Why will people put up with waistlines that don't fit because they ordered them from a catalog or spend dollars in gas and time to save pennies on cartons of cigarettes? Why are honest citizens willing to lie and ship clothing to false addresses in order to spare themselves sales tax? Tax shopping generates a frenzy of activity, not all of it logical.

Beneath all the noise there is a very serious conversation going on here, a conversation between a government and its people. Officials—town, county, state, and federal— regularly pretend to the world that they may choose the tax rate, and that their tax receipts will grow or shrink accordingly. This pretense is actually codified in American law and regulation—the technocrats call it "static analysis." Static analysis says that a 5 percent tax will bring in 5 percent of a certain revenue pool, and an 8 percent tax will bring in 8 percent. The crunchers don't consider asking whether that revenue pool will change in size. Most government officials write their budgets with such assumptions and expect the people to go along in the name of deficit reduction, necessities, or the general social good.

But people aren't automatons. And shoppers, who are also citizens and taxpayers, do react to avoid government's demands when they are able. In shopping, unlike other areas, they actually have a choice about taxation, even if it is a choice of saving a penny on a dollar. And the vigor with which they exercise this choice reflects the seriousness with which they question government and its taxes. They are saying, "This is too much." Or "This I won't take." Or "I will live with this, but only if something else compensates for it." They talk back to government by modifying their behavior—by buying less and thereby giving back less in tax to the government. The result is that the revenue officers very often find themselves disappointed with their take. If they want more revenue, they are going to have to listen to shoppers.

The conversation is not a new one. It dates back to the American Revolution, when Americans told the British they wouldn't stand for their sorts of taxes. Several of the founding fathers tried to figure out which taxes the new American citizens would live with. They thought a lot about excise taxes, one of the names for sales taxes. They thought that people would tolerate them better than other taxes. Alexander Hamilton praised these consumption taxes: "The amount to be contributed by each citizen will in a degree be at his own option, and can be regulated by an attention to his resources. The rich may be extravagant, the poor can be frugal; and private oppression may always be avoided by a judicious selection of objects proper for such impositions." He also wrote, "It is a signal advantage of taxes on articles of consumption that they contain in their own nature a security against excess." Government's excess, that is. Another thing that Hamilton liked about the excise taxes was that they were visible. People knew when they were encountering the greedy hand and could avoid it if they chose. So the young nation tried its excise-tax experiment, imposing, at different points, taxes on spirits and other goods.

A Reply from Citizens

It turned out that early Americans didn't *want* to encounter the greedy hand, even in the form of an excise tax. When the founding fathers levied their taxes on spirits and the like, America's early citizens talked back—with violence. During the Whiskey Rebellion, they picked up muskets and pitchforks. It was a bloody exchange between a people and their government, but a genuine one. Government listened, and by 1800 the United States, led by Thomas Jefferson, had given up on internal taxes altogether.

Today the descendants of those rebellions are the mild-mannered tax shoppers. And they, too, have an effect on their government, albeit a more moderate one. In 1992, for example, Minnesota was having budget problems. Lawmakers proposed introducing a sales tax on clothing. And why not? Minnesota's coffers badly needed one. But there was an outcry from citizens against the tax. Among the louder complainers were representatives of the then-new Mall of America. The lawmakers backed down.

At this writing, Minnesota is in surplus. Much of that surplus is due to the general prosperity of the nation. But some of it—a healthy share of it—comes from the Mall of America. Today the mall employs twelve thousand Minnesotans. Shoppers who spend at the Mall of America do pay tax—6.5 percent—on nonclothing items. That money has played a role in swelling the state's surplus. Today the state estimates that the megamall has had a $1.5 billion impact on the state. In this sense, Minnesota is a winner. It got the revenue that governments in North Dakota, South Dakota, Wisconsin, Manitoba, Bonn, and Tokyo lost.

New York's IKEA story provides another example of the

give-and-take. In the beginning, New York officials just sat back and watched with frustration as state and city lost much desired revenue to New Jersey. They were particularly unhappy that shoppers were traveling to New Jersey malls to buy clothing without paying sales tax. Then IKEA was so bold as to boast about the advantage in advertising, announcing "whopping" tax savings in advertisements it posted in New York. Finally, New York had a convenient scapegoat. James W. Wetzler, New York State's commissioner of taxation and finance, lashed out at the store. He was the official who sent staffers to copy down the license numbers of New York cars in IKEA's lot. Wetzler also threatened to subpoena delivery records for the tables, chairs, and garden furniture people bought at IKEA and had shipped to New York. But the news of these snoops also set off the shoppers. "First of all, I have a right to spend my own money where I want," Donna Currington, a thirty-three-year-old nurse from the Bronx told *The New York Times*. "That's the most ridiculous thing I ever heard," Lisa Halgren, a thirty-two-year-old Manhattanite, told the *Times* when it told her about New York's enforcement efforts. "I work hard. I pay taxes. If I want to save a little money, that's my business and no one else's."

IKEA retreated, confining its ad copy to vaguer talk about affordability. But so did New York. Fast-forward to the late 1990s, and IKEA is still benefiting New Jersey. And, even though transfusions from Wall Street have improved New York's fiscal health, the state is still facing shortfalls because shoppers travel to places like IKEA. New Yorkers are still angry about taxes. So angry that New York Health & Racquet Club, a local chain, publishes a series of ads under the title "Tax Break." The health club, of course, doesn't have the power to offer a tax break, just the simple price break, $300 off on a membership. But the copywriters recognized that New Yorkers are so hungry for tax relief that an advertisement mentioning the topic can sell gym memberships.

Finally, New York's mayor and governor started responding to the music. They announced an experiment: state and city would hold weeklong "tax holidays" on clothing purchases twice in a year's time. The consumers talked back—with tax-holiday spending sprees. Heartened, the lawmakers began to plan a broader and more permanent sales-tax decrease on clothing.

Governments, though, aren't always willing to give up their power. So they find ways to turn the tables on the tax game. One way they do this is by concealing their work, in the hopes that taxpayers won't react. This is why lawmakers don't break out what we pay in gas taxes on the gas pump. And it is why, whenever they introduce a new tax, they like to call it a charge, a fee, a license— anything other than a tax.

The Phone Tax

The most recent example of this came up when the Federal Communications Commission was planning a new tax on telephone calls. The tax was a high one—up to 5 percent on long distance calls. The goal of the tax was a noble one: funding the wiring of schools to the Internet. But the FCC guessed people didn't want to fund the wiring of schools, at least not to the tune of 5 percent a call. So it disguised its tax by calling it a "universal service charge." And the commission did its very best to conceal even that phrase from consumers. It begged major phone carriers like AT&T and Sprint to bury the cost in bills, not to itemize at all, so consumers wouldn't know what was driving up their costs. In the old days—before the breakup of AT&T in the early 1980s, this might have worked. AT&T did all sorts of favors for the federal government in exchange for the power to keep its national telephone monopoly.

But these aren't the old days. AT&T isn't a monopoly. The phone companies, all of them, must operate in a competitive market. AT&T, Sprint, and MCI were legitimately afraid they would lose customers if they didn't explain the new cost to customers. Eventually—after an enormous fight—they prevailed and itemized the tax on monthly statements. The FCC began to hem and haw about the size of its tax, even talked about reducing it. It seemed the invisible hand might get the better of the greedy hand, at least for the moment.

Meanwhile, though, the greedy hand, always on the lookout for new pockets, was busy elsewhere. As soon as Internet shopping took wing in the mid-1990s, state revenue departments got to work trying to find a way to tax it. The state of Ohio was the most aggressive of the tax collectors. But Americans didn't like the notion of tax coming to their Internet lives, an area that had heretofore seemed blissfully free of government intervention. They complained. Eventually Congress passed, and President Clinton signed, the Internet freedom bill, severely curtailing Web taxation.

Over the years state lawmakers and those who levy shopping taxes have become cleverer about this. They have figured out that the greedy hand can keep its control—and

continue to jerk citizens around—if it dispenses tax *favors*.
The Mall of America's tax financing was one such example.
Elizabeth, New Jersey's, special urban-enterprise zone is
another one.

Taxpayers shouldn't necessarily welcome these changes.
That's because many of them end up losers in the game.
Minnesota's losers are the citizens of Minneapolis and St.
Paul, who pay more to subsidize the breaks the state gives
to Bloomington's Mall of America. They are the purchasers
of furniture, batteries, cars—anything but clothing or
food—who subsidize the citizens who make those tax-free
purchases of clothing and food. Over the years this form of
patronage has become very expensive: states spend hundreds of millions to lure particular businesses. That's a form
of corporate welfare that hurts a silent majority who don't
have a lobby to pound doors at the state office for industrial
development.

The Case of Cigarettes

Today this has particular relevance, because in coming
years America will see one of the greater experiments in tax
shopping in our history. Federal and state lawmakers have
joined hands to raise tobacco taxes, an effort to gain revenue by punishing a behavior we've come to know is dangerous: smoking. But if they raise tobacco taxes too much,
people will react. They will manufacture bootleg cigarettes
here. Or they will cross the border to buy cigarettes off the
books in Mexico, or pay runners and smugglers who will do
that for them.

Canada ran such an experiment when it raised cigarette
taxes in 1991. Soon there was massive smuggling, which led

to terrible crime and a general breakdown of order. The Mounties were called out: the government took to running elaborate sting operations. But not all provinces went along. Bruce Bartlett, an economist who studied the matter, noted that a carton of cigarettes can be bought for $26.40 Canadian (U.S. $18.50) in Ontario and resold illegally for $48.55 in British Columbia or $50.62 in Newfoundland. A new round of smuggling ensued. The papers reported that enough cigarettes were being smuggled into British Columbia to feed the habits of 130,000 smokers.

To those who say that can't happen in America, the sobering answer is that it already has. In the 1930s, Prohibition's constraints on the sale of liquor showed how angry citizens can become when government intrudes too much on the matter of their sin. The result was the greatest lawlessness of this century. While heavy cigarette taxes are not the same as an outright ban, they too are likely to do wonders for the underground sale and smuggling of the punished commodity.

Meanwhile the tax game goes on, move and countermove, an amusing exercise but also a grim one. To know what it means to consumers, one has only to talk to people who plan trips to the Mall of America, or look at the faces of the parents filing under the blue-and-yellow awning of IKEA stores. They are excited, but they are also determined. Their expressions seem to say that their bargain better be there at the other end, their excursion had better deliver the excitement and the savings they hope for. They have come this far, and they are determined that they are going to get something back.

3

YOUR WORK

Bureaucrats are no different from other people. They want to be appreciated. When, in recent years, the press began calling our Social Security system a trick, a fraud, and worse, the civil servants at the Social Security Administration were put out. They grew furious when the papers repeatedly compared their beloved employer to the Ponzi scheme, a legendary fraud on investors orchestrated by the 1920s con man Charles Ponzi. Eventually, some of the Social Security employees moved to revolt. Larry DeWitt, the administration's official historian, penned a fierce assault on the smears and posted it in a corner of the administration's Web site labeled "History Myths."

DeWitt's rebuttal of the Ponzi claim was a beautiful thing. First he mounted a picture of Charles Ponzi, complete with period mustache and pomade. Then DeWitt explained how Ponzi lured investors with promises of tempting returns on foreign postal coupons. In reality, of course, the investors weren't investing in the coupons. They were investing in each other. The plan was a pyramid scheme. Money from the second generation of buyers simply flowed into the accounts of the first generation. The whole thing worked smoothly, just like a chain letter. The only problem was that Ponzi eventually ran out of takers. And when he ran out of takers, Ponzi ran out of "returns." Investors, courts, and judges turned on Ponzi with a vengeance so strong he ended up begging President Coolidge for the mercy of "immediate deportation" from a Houston jailhouse.

Next DeWitt devoted some space to reviewing the mathematical nature of Ponzi's scheme. Ponzi's arrangement, he noted, was a geometric progression, one that "works only so long as there is an ever-increasing number of new investors coming into the scheme." But Social Security, he pointed out, was a simple arithmetic progression: one person pays in, another takes out. "There is nothing unsavory about such a system," DeWitt concluded vehemently, "and it is sustainable forever, provided that the number of new people entering the system maintains a rough balance with the number of people collecting from the system." This is surely true, as long as the economy and demography cooperate.

The Fantasy

But the economy and demography haven't cooperated, which is what makes Social Security indeed and truly a Ponzi scheme. In fact, the troubles of the program that we hear about so frequently today are not surprising ones. Long ago actuaries could foresee what would happen to Social Security: even planners in the 1950s knew it. It has taken much longer, until deep into the 1990s, for most of the nation to begin to see what the planners comprehended all along: Social Security is a fantasy. A comforting, pleasant fantasy, one that has sustained many millions of Americans over the decades, but a fantasy all the same.

Here's how it all came about. Washington promised, from the start, that Social Security would be a trust: a trust that invested and then returned Social Security money to Social Security recipients. In reality, there was no trust. There was merely cash flow. Cash came in from contributors and went out the same day to senior citizens. This was the root of the deception.

Today the economy is growing, so the money is still coming in. And the baby boomers are still working. Because more people are paying in than are taking out, the Social Security budget is in surplus. This means that current retirees and those a little younger will get their money, at least for a while. To their eyes, therefore, Social Security seems to live up to its official title of "trust." They don't generally mind paying payroll taxes—the money from their paycheck that goes to Social Security and Medicare. They look at the letters FICA, letters that stand for Federal Insurance Contributions Act, and then they look away. If they see Social Security as a tax at all, they see it as a "good tax," a sort of "untax" whose costs it seems worthwhile to carry. In general, though, these people are reluctant to think about Social Security. In their mind payroll taxes are minor things that live in the shadow of the mighty income tax. They can say to themselves that their Social Security really was not a tax, but a down payment into the trust, a promise of a pension on the other side of their working lives. Medicare, the second payroll tax, was also a commitment to a certain reward: health care in a fragile old age. Somehow, the whole problem seems to them best unexamined.

These, though, are the members of a privileged cohort.

Younger people face a different situation. These taxpayers are now confronting the following fact: around 2012, the pot will move into deficit. And around 2030, when the later baby boomers and Generation X'ers will want to think about collecting their money, the pot will begin to look empty. The economy is growing, but it isn't growing fast enough to fund everyone through decades of retirement. And, as important, there won't be enough younger workers to pay all the necessary money into the system. If 1990s lawmakers hadn't written such restrictive immigration laws, this might not be such a problem. But the miniwave of nativism that overcame them and led them to curtail the inflow of workers insured that our Social Security challenge will be acute. The pot simply won't contain enough to pay the pensions of people who retire after 2035—people who are under thirty now. Medicare, too, will not survive the budgetary challenges these generations are set to impose on it. These people's "trust" is not a trust. It is not even an untax. It is a real tax, a tax dedicated to an uncertain reward.

This is something that most of the younger crowd have divined by now. One study—mentioned almost as frequently as the tired Ponzi story—shows that more young people believe in UFOs than believe they will get their money when the time comes. But younger people, too, have trouble taking to the streets over Social Security. Their position is rather one of angry incomprehension—similar to that grand sticker shock forced on them by withholding. To understand the general frustration, it helps to suspend all our preconceptions—the big myths—and look at the program from their point of view.

The challenge begins with payroll taxes' very scale. For younger people, the central tax is not income tax, it is FICA, which looms on their paycheck stubs like a *Tyrannosaurus rex*. To them Social Security is a job tax, indeed *the* job tax, the major tax fact of the first decade of their career life. This problem is not confined to entry-level workers. For an astounding seven out of ten American households, the payroll tax is the greatest of all taxes they pay.

Part of the reason there's been no outcry over this is that half of the payroll tax is hidden from workers' view. The pay stub says that payroll taxes equal 7.65 percent. But that 7.65 percent that the employee sees represents only half his load. Employers must match the employee contribution with another 7.65 percent, which they pay on their employees' behalf. Businesses being what they are—mere sieves through which monies flow—it is not the businesses who lose here. The employees are the ones who lose, for they forgo that amount in wages. Employers give that 7.65 percent to the government instead of to the employee. The real rate on payroll taxes, as employment taxes are sometimes called, is 15.3 percent. That means someone earning $50,000 surrenders more than $7,500 a year to what is universally acknowledged to be a faltering system. And people pay that kind of money on every dollar of their first $70,000 in income.

Then there is the structure of the tax. The $70,000 cap is an important one. That's where Social Security stops. Every dollar people earn after the $70,000 limit is a dollar they can collect without funding the Ponzi scheme. That's nice for higher earners. But it also means that, in economists' terms, the payroll tax is that thing we have not ever, in the history of the century, allowed the income tax to be: it is regressive.

By their nature, then, payroll taxes are a worker's tax, a

tax on getting started, a tax that encumbers students and young people who have made the commitment to work and are now learning what that commitment requires. They are also a tax on minorities and immigrants just beginning their American lives. The very group our lawmakers so frequently talk about helping through taxes is the group hit hardest by payroll taxes: families earning between $20,000 and $50,000.

Burdened Soldiers

The soldiers who shoulder the untax's burden are entry-level workers, people like McDonald's crew hands, who earn $6 or $7 an hour. Now that welfare has lost its charm as a policy solution, Washington has concentrated on exhorting these workers to stay on the job, from time to time forcing hikes in the minimum wage or encouraging them through various breaks on income tax. But the workers must still pay a flat 7.65 percent in FICA on even the first dollar they earn.

Economists write about this all the time, but it still comes as a shock to those setting out in life. In the winter of 1998 a college student who had worked a summer job came to me for help in getting a tax refund. He had a form, a 1099-MISC, showing he had earned $5,000 for his summer's work at a law firm, an impressive amount but well below the minimum required to pay income tax these days. The fellow wasn't due a refund at all. Because his employer hadn't withheld FICA, he actually owed hundreds of dollars—something he wasn't prepared for. Still, he seemed willing to pay this contribution, his contribution—"that insurance." The same burden falls on those less equipped to carry it than the student—part-time earners around the poverty line. This group pays no income tax, but it does pay Social Security.

The untax also hits job generators like small businesses, which are often virtual FICA-collection machines. McDonald's did an interesting study of selected franchisees, blacks and Hispanics who were the first in their families to go into such businesses. It found that the franchisees' average tax bill before paying FICA was something like 40 percent, well above the American average. After paying FICA their total tax load rose to 60 percent or more.

One of the McDonald's examples was a Florida family named Rodriguez, a family that had fled Castro. Angel Rodriguez, the father, bought his first McDonald's restaurant in 1980. In fifteen years, he and his family built up the business to seven restaurants. His wife, Gladys, worked in the office. His son Alex was his partner. Another son, Roy, supervised three stores. A daughter, Vivian, managed the office. Even his father, Roberto, worked in the business before he became too ill with Parkinson's disease, handing out napkins and jollying customers at one of the restaurants.

What was important here was that this family actually felt it had little need for the government's insurance. The Rodriguezes were, in an important sense, their own insurance. They took care of one another by giving one another jobs. Yet each of these people took home less from their family jobs because they were paying their share of FICA. And for each of the family members, Angel, the founder, paid FICA too. That meant he could pay family members less. It even made it harder for him to "insure"—to hire—family members.

The payroll tax also prevented the Rodriguezes from

helping people outside their family. They bought health insurance for the twenty managers they employ. But theirs was, after all, a small business; its restaurants were situated cheek by jowl with Kentucky Fried Chicken, Burger King, and Taco Bell. The FICA cost meant they could not afford to do things they would like to do for their employees. Angel Rodriguez wanted to buy health insurance for all his employees, but in 1998 he told me that he could not—FICA and other taxes were just too high. He wished he had resources left in his budget, but with the costs of FICA, especially the Medicare, "there's no room left."

Most people know somehow that the FICA bite is bigger than the official 7.65 percent, or even the 15.3 percent, but they have trouble explaining to themselves why that is so. The answer is a technical reason: FICA money is taxed twice. Taxpayers first pay FICA on their gross income. Then they pay income tax on the income, as if the FICA money had never been taken out. Economists call this "double taxation" and write essays about the phenomenon. Average taxpayers just know that the bottom line feels smaller than it ought to, sometimes much smaller.

Women Lose

There is a group that loses still more than others in the Social Security arrangement—women. Ann Thomas, a tax expert who teaches at New York Law School, points out that married women who work are big losers. That is because Social Security is based on the principle of one pension per household. When husbands retire, they get benefits. If they are married, the pair gets an even greater benefit. But that benefit is typically based on the higher earner's contribution, not on any smaller contribution a second earner, usually a woman, might have made. In other words, the fact that a woman has worked and paid into Social Security for years, sometimes a number of years, may ease her retirement not at all. The money married women pay into Social Security often does not make it back to them.

No matter. Today feeding the FICA beast has become a national pastime. Some 130 million Americans pay into the Social Security system, or around 35 million more than the number who chose to vote in the 1996 presidential elections. Most Americans start work around the age of twenty, and Social Security's actuaries bank on them working until age sixty-two, sixty-five, sixty-seven, or older. Every year workers pay some $350 billion into Social Security. The Ponzi engine is bigger than it has ever been. In 1950, social insurance taxes, the category that includes such things as Medicare and Social Security, were 11 percent of all the money the federal government took in; in 1997 they were 36 percent. In 1996 the government collected $476.3 billion in various FICA-type employment taxes from working people, a sum not so very much less than the $656.4 billion it extracted in individual income tax.

The Greatest Gift

This is a social cost that dwarfs the welfare system of the 1960s, 1970s, and 1980s. Americans who came of age in the 1960s and 1970s are the protagonists in this drama. In this decade alone, baby boomers and X'ers will hand trillions to Americans born before 1940. This largely unsung act is the

greatest public transfer of wealth—and the greatest gift—
from one group to another documented in American history.

It is easy to see how this state of affairs came about. Nobody, particularly no politician, wants to develop a reputation for fiddling with a national trust. Then there is another
fact: our nation's political leaders never had to pay Social
Security in precisely the way lower earners now pay it.
When they were young, FICA was a small tax. When a pair
Bill and Hillary Clinton's age, or George W. Bush's, was
starting out, FICA payments were capped at income levels
below $8,000. Even when the tax moved up, it did not affect
this elite. The raising of the cap to $70,000 was recent, and
the full impact of that change didn't hit our nation's leaders
and the more successful of the media that cover them.
That's because by the time the change came along, many
of them earned *above* the cap. American lawmakers' *average* Social Security tax rate is well below that of lower
earners—thanks to regressivity. They have never known
and will never know the FICA burden that the average
American shoulders.

And it is easy to see why seniors went along with it. In the
1960s and 1970s, Washington expanded benefits so frequently that seniors saw very respectable rates of return on
their Social Security money. Nobody pointed out to them
that by taking generous payments from the program, they
were cutting benefits for those who followed. It would have
been very impolitic.

But what about the rest of Americans, the generations of people who pay the full load decade after decade?
How the baby boomers and X'ers landed this role is some-
what of a mystery. They are, after all, the 1968 and *Ally*

McBeal crowd, groups whose claim to fame is their rejection of authority, their narcissism, and their materialism. Why, one has to ask, is the generation that so famously rejected responsibility acting so conscientiously, so masochistically? One possible answer to the mystery is that the baby boomers and Generation X'ers pay the money out of simple generosity. In other words, they like to see what Social Security gives their parents.

There is a second explanation. It is that baby boomers, at least the younger ones, have left Social Security alone because someone told them to do that. And that someone is an authority they actually do respect, all rebellious posturing notwithstanding. It is their parents. Any talk of reform means change. Change means risking the benefits that currently flow to senior citizens, who are, after all, one's own aging and vulnerable relatives. Then of course there is the fear, faintly illogical, that these parents might indeed lose benefits and need more help from their own flesh and blood—in other words, the baby boomers. All material for a dinner-table conversation that everyone involved in wants to avoid.

There is a third and powerful reason for our reflexive protectiveness of Social Security. It is that Social Security is part of the bedrock of the twentieth century, the foundation of history on which we imagine ourselves standing as a people. Questioning Social Security seems to mean questioning government, not just its recent decisions but more primal decisions made as far back as the New Deal. Taking on Social Security in some way or other means taking on Franklin Roosevelt himself, a step tantamount for many to intellectual treason. And this is something many

Americans, Republican or Democrat, are simply not prepared to do. How can someone who hasn't been through the Depression, as our oldest citizens have, question what was necessary in that Depression? Every young person who asks about programs like Social Security has had the experience of being chastised: "You don't know what it was like in the Depression." Most of us would rather suspend disbelief about Social Security. It is easier to nurse some kind of attenuated faith that, if only we deliver our share of the Social Security bargain, the program will find a way to return the favor when our time comes.

A Visit to the SSA

To know the hold of the Social Security fantasy it helps to pay a visit to the wonderland itself—the Social Security Administration. A low white edifice cast in the no-name architecture of the late 1950s, it sits in Baltimore's outlands, emanating the comforting promise of safety and protection. To get there one must travel a road called Security Boulevard. One must follow several signs reading TO SOCIAL SECURITY ADMINISTRATION and pass—of all places—Security Square Mall. Once inside, the visitor confronts a rather elaborate checking system—Security, again—requiring the completion of a full-page form before entrance is granted. The bespectacled, cardiganed people who work here have a cautious, sweet look, as if they actually sought out their jobs in the first place because they liked the idea of an employer whose name includes the word *security*.

Until all the recent affronts to their institutional person, the civil servants here have had another reason to feel warm. Every month they pass out funds to 43 million people, the beneficiaries of Social Security. Of those, 7.4 million—widows, widowers, and orphans—receive $5.2 billion each year. Knowing this gives Social Security employees something rarely given to government bureaucrats: the chance to feel lovable. They walk their rust-colored carpets with the confidence that they are a bureaucracy with a heart, a proud and explicit contrast to their bloodless brethren at the IRS.

The idea that it is somehow right for the government to protect America's old people did not start with the New Deal. Even in the very early days of the republic there were cries for some organized, official form of support for older people. The Social Security Administration's Baltimore building is a no-nonsense place, a sort of giant backroom office for numbers processing. But it does have a one-room museum, in which hangs a suggestion for an early version of Social Security offered by none other than Thomas Paine. Writing in a 1795 pamphlet titled *Agrarian Justice,* he suggested that Britain raise inheritance taxes to sustain its aged. In those days it was families and churches to whom older people turned for help. Paine, though, saw that God, or at least the god of King George's England, was not delivering. He wanted the government to take over the job. Under Paine's plan, the government would assure "Ten Pounds Sterling per Annum during the life of every Person now living of the Age of *fifty* years and to all others when they shall arrive at that Age to enable them to live in Old Age without Wretchedness and go decently out of the World."

"Need for Security"

When the moment of our own national "wretchedness" arrived—the Great Depression—Americans for the first time demanded security from their government. One in four workers was unemployed. More than a quarter of families lost their homes. Very few people had private pensions. "Need for Security," read the report title of the Committee on Economic Security, a group assigned by President Franklin Roosevelt to come up with a solution. Approximately eighteen million Americans were dependent upon emergency relief at the moment they took up the problem. "There is insecurity at every stage of life," wrote the federal commission. President Roosevelt, like Paine, felt that government must step in to do work formerly done in the privacy of church and family. Congress agreed: the House passed the Social Security Act by 372–33 votes, and the Senate by 77–6. When Roosevelt signed the Federal Insurance Contributions Act in 1935, he explained that help was needed because of the retreat of the old agricultural order. "The civilization of the past hundred years with its startling industrial changes has tended more and more to make life insecure. Young people have come to wonder what would be their lot when they came to old age."

In 1936 the new Social Security Board laid out its promise to the nation in a pamphlet with the understated title *Informational Circular Number 9*. "Beginning November 24, 1936, the United States will set up a Social Security account for you," the circular began with compelling fanfare. "There is now a law in this country which will give about 26 million working people something to live on when they are old and have stopped working," the pamphlet continued. "This means that if you work in some factory, shop, mine, mill, store, office, or almost any other kind of business or industry, you will be earning benefits that will come to you later on."

"The Most You Will Ever Have to Pay"

The board did something else that resounds today. It assured American workers that "the checks will come to you as your right"—a "right," not simply an entitlement, a program, or a benefit. It made another unusual, daring move. It promised the workers that there would be limits on what they would have to pay in. Even a decade hence, the authors write, "You and your employer will each pay 3 cents on each dollar you earn, up to $3,000," with a confidence that would be hard to imagine coming from the obfuscatory Washington of today. And it concluded with a reverberating promise: "That is the most you will ever have to pay."

When the Social Security Administration began cutting checks, it publicized the name of the very first recipient of its early payments. It started with lump-sum benefits to seniors who were retiring just as the program began, and the first applicant for such benefit was a Cleveland train motorman, Ernest Ackerman. Mr. Ackerman worked one day within the Social Security program—the day the program began—and then retired. The government withheld five cents from that day's pay and then gave him a lump-sum retirement benefit of seventeen cents.

The first recipient of regular monthly payments was Ida May Fuller, a Ludlow, Vermont, spinster with the upholstered look typical of the period. Miss Fuller received her

first monthly check on January 31, 1940. The amount was
$22.54. Miss Fuller, the Social Security Administration
archives show, lived to age one hundred, getting back a
total of $22,888.92, far more than she had ever put in. Miss
Fuller's picture was a staple in Social Security Administration publicity in the 1940s and 1950s, Exhibit A in the
administration's evidence that it would stick to its promise.

Yet from the start Social Security was not really the arrangement it pretended to be. No single individual had an
"account," as FDR had promised. There was no trust,
where the money rested untouched. The surpluses workers
paid in were borrowed by the federal government, traded
for government bonds. Critics of Social Security were quick
to perceive this. On the wall of the office of the Social Security Administration's historian hangs a framed copy of a
1938 headline from the *Boston American.* It reads: HERE'S
PROOF OF DECEIT IN PAYROLL TAX, MONEY NOT SET ASIDE
IN PENSIONS.

Living with the Fiction

People chose to live with this fiction, their myth, for a long
time, longer than the working life of most Americans. They
did this because, for those years, the Social Security Administration delivered. It delivered to retired men. It delivered
to their wives and their children. It delivered them far more
than they had ever paid in. It delivered so well that it did
a rare thing, for a federal program—it begat copycat
programs. In 1965 President Johnson leaned on the Social
Security example to rally support for creating Social Security's sibling, Medicare, which guaranteed universal health
insurance for Americans over sixty-five.

By the 1970s Social Security inspired such faith that it was asked to apply its golden touch to entirely separate programs. Supplemental Security Income, the program that serves the blind and disabled, sounds like it is part of Social Security. And the program is indeed administered by the Social Security Administration. But it is actually funded from tax revenues and as such is not really part of Social Security at all. Today a wide range of social-insurance projects live under Social Security's big umbrella. A 1996 pamphlet from the administration, "Social Security: Basic Facts," shows that sixty-nine cents of every FICA dollar pay retirement and survivor benefits. Nineteen cents go to Medicare, and twelve cents go to pay disability.

Social Security's defenders, and there are still quite a few, continue to enumerate the program's virtues. The first, a not insignificant one, is that it is efficient—the entire program is manned by a relatively small bureaucracy of 60,000, in contrast to the more than 100,000 at the IRS. Unlike the income tax, which sometimes seems to collect revenue simply to show that it can, Social Security's is a dedicated program, one that gives people a clear understanding of what they are paying the tax for. Bob Gleason, a Social Security Administration civil servant who researches how Americans feel about Social Security, notes that individuals rarely complain about the program. That is because, he says, it's not an abstraction to them. Most people know someone who gets Social Security. Even Milton Friedman, one of the earliest Social Security cynics, commented that the direct link between the taxation and the benefits was very powerful. "The two combined have become a sacred cow," he said in 1971. "What a triumph of imaginative packaging and Madison Avenue advertising."

People also like the fact that Social Security has been predictable. Unlike the federal tax code, Social Security has seen only seven major changes in its half century of history. And its bureaucrats work hard to please their customers, demanding senior citizens, by cushioning them to even the tiniest of changes.

Check Day

A story about "check day" provides a good example of this. For decades, recipients received their Social Security checks on the third of the month. This created a cycle of rush and panic for the folks at Security Boulevard, who faithfully predelivered the checks to the post office so that citizens could be certain their money would arrive on the right day. At one point the Social Security Administration thought it might try to diminish the chaos by staggering the dates of delivery. But when it queried its "customers"—senior citizens—in focus groups, they weren't keen on the change. So the officials in Baltimore settled on a compromise that seemed acceptable to everyone. It would stagger dates for new recipients but "grandfather" those already accustomed to the old arrangement.

The result of all this solicitousness is that the morale at Security Boulevard is far higher than anything at the ghoulish IRS. Social Security Administration employees care for their beneficiaries, and they care for one another. For a while the Social Security Administration Web site, SSA.gov, carried a page titled "Social Security's Greatest Tragedy," commemorating each of the sixteen Social Security Administration employees who died in the 1995 bomb explosion of the Alfred P. Murrah Federal Building in Oklahoma City.

Whenever outsiders question Social Security, and lately they have done so more and more frequently, the program has reacted with all the loyalty and outrage of a law-abiding dowager. Its public-affairs offices have worked hard to justify Washington's decision to repeatedly ask working voters to pay a bigger share, far more than the government originally promised. It has defended the new high levels of income subject to the payroll tax. It has built up the arguments on its Web site.

The Collapse Ahead

By now it is clear to everyone, even the non–Generation X'ers, that Social Security's myth is about to collapse. The first reason this is true is a problem the administration's soulful actuaries long foresaw but could do nothing about. Life expectancy at the beginning of the decade in which Social Security was created was fifty-eight years old, or younger than the age entitled to achieve benefits. Americans now live into their late seventies. Then there is the issue of the baby boom, a curve on the birthrate chart that ends so abruptly one is forced to appreciate the social revolution brought by the arrival of the birth control pill. When the baby boomers hit retirement, there simply won't be the same number of workers to support them.

The most recent alert on this came in 1996, when the Social Security Advisory Commission, a group that makes its report every four years, noted that the current surplus in funds would run out in 2012 and that the system would require much higher taxes after that point. One of the best depictions of the problem came from Laurence Kotlikoff, a professor at Boston University who does leading work in a branch of economics known as generational accounting. He noted that while Americans currently carry an average tax burden of something like 30 percent, that figure will have to move to 50 percent if future generations are to sustain the baby boomers in retirement. In other words, the generous baby boomers must turn their successors into tax slaves if they are to collect on the scale that their parents did.

Better Returns

There are some simple solutions to this. One would be to tinker some more by raising the age of payout to seventy. Another would be to further cap or tax the benefits to the wealthy. A third would be to raise the cap on what workers pay into the system. These, though, would be a betrayal for a simple reason. Social Security may be a good deal, but it is not the best deal for citizens.

In the 1990s, a second and powerful argument against Social Security has made that clear. It is the argument that the market can do better. This idea, of course, pleases Wall Street, which has long lusted after the billions in Social Security's coffers. So mutual funds and investment banks have pushed this angle, contributing to think tanks, generating books, and sending speakers out into the world in the hopes of capturing the billions of Social Security dollars that now go to the U.S. government.

Wall Street's motives may well be obvious, but its case is

a compelling one. William Shipman, an advocate of Social Security privatization from the giant Boston investment firm State Street Global Advisors, lays out some scenarios. His first example is a twenty-six-year-old computer programmer—or any other young high earner—who is allowed to stick half of his Social Security tax payments into a personal stock fund. Fast-forward through perhaps two thousand such weekly payments. A lifetime of such investing will give the computer programmer a monthly pension that is the equivalent of $5,864 in 1995 dollars. The other half of the money will yield only $984 a month. An equally generous pension also awaits those lower down on the income scale, including the emblematic McDonald's workers. Men and women born in 1970, who earn half the average national wage, a mere $12,600 a year, are the people who are supposed to need Social Security. Under mid-1990s law, they are entitled to a monthly payment of $769 when they retire. That figure would more than triple, moving up to $2,419 a month, if they could place a career's worth of monthly payments into stocks.

By this argument even the senior citizens who are getting the full benefit of Social Security—the fortunate ones, demographically speaking—have lost a lot by sticking with their dowager. Her investment, "the safest of all possible investments," as it is called in some of the administration literature, is not as safe as it would be in the risky stock market. The State Street numbers crunchers also studied a sixty-six-year-old whose long career entitled him to a monthly $1,200. Had that money been invested in stocks over his lifetime, he would be starting his retirement on $3,999 in Social Security monies each month.

Most important, the numbers here aren't pretending that every decade will be a bull decade like the 1980s and 1990s. They are based on an average annual return of stocks of 10 percent, below what we have seen in recent decades. The numbers are still dramatic if you assume an average return of 7 percent.

Other firms have calculated average annual returns over a longer period, including the dreary market of the 1960s and even the 1930s. The gist of the message is that the payout on market investment is so outstanding that it leaves room for any number of giant "corrections." When the Cato Institute, a conservative think tank, calculated the numbers, it found that even investors who had stayed in the stock market through the Great Depression did better, over a lifetime, than they would have had they had their money in the sort of investment offered to Americans by Social Security.

Minority Advantage

The Washington-based Heritage Foundation has done work on what this change could mean for minorities. Black men are in a difficult situation, since the average black male lives only to the age of sixty-one. That means that while he works his entire life putting money into Social Security, he often does not get any payback. His widow may get his Social Security pension. But his children cannot inherit it. Low-income black males born after 1959 actually face a negative rate of return on their contributions. For every dollar they put in, they get only eighty-eight cents back. When this data hit the media, African-Americans responded with excitement. Think-tank economists went on black talk radio. Their op-eds appeared in African-American newspapers. What the black community liked about their work was precisely the emphasis it placed on returning wealth and control to the family. The Heritage numbers showed that putting Social Security money into an investment composed half of Treasury bills and half of stocks would give a rate of return of something like 5 percent to this group. If that money were in a private account—say, an individual retirement account—then parents who died early could pass the money along to their children. A private pension would also address the working woman's problems.

Critics argue that Americans aren't ready for such a change. What, they ask, about the people who don't save? The answer is that people would have individual accounts, but they wouldn't have access to them: a privatized Social Security plan is something like a mandatory and inaccessible IRA. When retirement time came, then they would get access. But that could be structured something like a monthly annuity: the nest egg payout wouldn't come all at once.

The critics also worry that citizens will invest badly. In the 1980s, Japan looked to be an unbeatable model. Very few of the experts who invested there foresaw the catastrophes awaiting the tsunami economy. How then could one expect normal citizens to predict the failures of Japanese banks, or the gymnastics of the Indonesian rupiah, for that matter? The answer, one already proposed by lawmakers such as Senator Phil Gramm, is that privatized money could go into limited, balanced funds. In many cases, the rewards of partial privatization look to be far greater than the risks.

Indeed, the nation today is well positioned to privatize Social Security "safely." Just ten years ago our deficit was so wide that there was no question of there being "extra" funds around at the Treasury to dedicate to a Social Security project. Today, by contrast, we are looking at federal surpluses. Martin Feldstein of the National Bureau of Economic Research has proposed a neat solution: use the extra money from general tax revenues to provide the basis for citizens' new accounts. That way, their participation in the old program will go unchanged. The money that grows in the privatized accounts will simply be an extra, an add-on, a much desired bonus.

There is a danger contained in the new privatization passion. Many of the "privatization" plans currently being touted for Social Security aren't true privatization. These plans would indeed set aside a share of individuals' payroll taxes in separate stock and bond market accounts. But they would also have government oversee those accounts—even guaranteeing them. If these funds fail, even momentarily, the government may well feel compelled to "rescue them." A Social Security "rescue" would dwarf other rescues in our recent history, costing, for example, many hundreds of billions more than the famous 1980s Savings and Loan bailout. And if the accounts grow fast, there is another problem—they will become too tempting for politicians. For what is to stop lawmakers from treating these new "accounts" the same way they treated the old Social Security "trust"—as their own? In the name of privatization, politicians would actually be passing laws that expanded government. It's a real concern, particularly when considered in the context of the national experience with Social Security thus far.

In any case, all this heated privatization talk troubles the Social Security Administration's soul. But it does not prevent the administration from assigning blame elsewhere, spinning facts when possible, and generally defending itself like crazy. In public speeches featured on the administration's Web site in the spring of 1998, Kenneth S. Apfel, the Social Security commissioner, announced that the program's trust funds would be fully exhausted by the year 2029, that his agency was reacting in a statesmanly fashion, but that it was the job of Congress to prevent crisis.

One thing is certain. The very last place to come to grips with this necessity will be the Social Security Administration itself.

The same Web site that contains the famous Ponzi rebuttal also includes an elaborate and quite attractive set of pages for teenagers. In the teen section, the question of Social Security's future is treated a little differently. To be sure, the site's creators boldly post their question: "Will Social Security be there for you?" But they supply a much softer answer than Mr. Apfel's. "Most people," they note in politic tone, "agree that Social Security will be there for you when you are ready to retire in the distant future. The real question is what will be its shape."

Yet when the Social Security officials came to the task of constructing a page for the very youngest of readers, children who will become senior citizens long after the dreaded 2029 cutoff, they changed their pitch. Beside a curly-tailed cyber pig, the Social Security authors posted large childish letters reading: "Social Security is your piggy bank to the future." Then, as if unable to face what they knew, the authors reverted to blank denial. In a headline above the pig, they posted, yet again, the old unkeepable promise: "Social Security will be there for you when you need it."

4

YOUR MARRIAGE

IN THE SPRING OF 1997 THE STAFFERS WHO OPENED THE
mail for an Indiana congressman named Dave McIntosh
came across an amazing thing. McIntosh, a Republican,
had been looking into a problem known as the marriage
penalty. Under the contorted and complicated rules of the
tax code, married couples often found that they were paying
more tax than they would on the same income if they were
single. McIntosh had heard a lot about the marriage
penalty, so much that he was at work crafting legislation to
stop it.

The letter came from a couple who faced the marriage
penalty, Darryl Pierce and Sharon Mallory of Straughn, Indiana. The pair had been living together for some time.
They both worked making radiators at the Ford Electronics
plant in Connersville; Sharon worked on assembly and
Darryl was a machine operator. They duly did what many
couples in America now do when they consider a serious
question like matrimony: they went to their accountant.
The lady behind the desk in New Castle confirmed that
the pair would indeed face a tremendous marriage penalty. Now, as a single woman, Sharon was receiving a

$900-a-year refund on her taxes. Getting married would mean she and Darryl would lose the refund. They would instead find themselves writing the IRS a check for $2,800.

What made this letter unusual was that Darryl and Sharon weren't merely complaining. They were actually making an important personal decision based on the marriage penalty—they were putting off their wedding. "Now there is nothing right about this," wrote Sharon in her letter to McIntosh. "After we continually hear the government preach to us about 'family values.' " Later in the letter, Sharon turned reflective. "Darryl and I would very much like to be married, and I must say it broke our hearts when we found out we can't afford it."

McIntosh, one of the members of the famous class of Republican freshmen in the 104th Congress, was an ambitious man. Later the same year, after the Speaker of the House, Newt Gingrich, announced his retirement, McIntosh's would be among the names put forward for the Speaker job. Now he found himself getting serious about the marriage penalty. He himself had recently married. His wife, Ruthie, had worked on Barbara Bush's staff in the White House. McIntosh started mentioning the way the tax punished working couples in his speeches. He thought this story would dramatize the marriage-penalty issue enough to win significant support from fellow Republicans and even some Democrats—one of Sharon's favorite politicians was David Bonior, whose anti-NAFTA views she, as a factory worker, vigorously supported. So McIntosh posted the letter from Indiana on his Web site, along with other E-mail from couples. He arranged for Sharon and Darryl to come to Washington to testify. And he set about developing marriage-penalty legislation that would allow Darryl and

Sharon to continue to enjoy the beneficial tax status they had as singles even after they married.

A Suitable Project

For McIntosh, marriage-penalty reform had a signal advantage: it was the right size. Republicans knew that President Clinton, a Democrat, would not go for a large, Reagan-style tax reform. "Fixing" the marriage penalty looked to be a project small enough that the president might sign off on it. And it was important, because the tax did affect many Americans. A government study had recently shown that 21 million American couples paid an average marriage penalty of $1,400. All Republicans, whether they were centrists, free-market types, or social conservatives, knew that a project that helped the family budget would be very popular. Undoing the marriage penalty seemed ambitious yet manageable. It seemed possible.

McIntosh won backing for marriage-penalty legislation from Gingrich, and from the chairman of the House Ways and Means Committee, Bill Archer. His bill even had support from a group that had become important to the party in the 1990s, the Christian Coalition. The coalition's president, Don Hodel, endorsed the plan, saying, "This legislation places government on the side of families."

Shaping Marriages

The tax experts tended to look at the marriage penalty as an irksome technicality, a problem that arose from a variety of arcane accounting details. In the case of Sharon and Darryl, they noted that the couple might not be losing so much if

Darryl didn't have a son from an earlier relationship. They wouldn't lose so much if Sharon weren't earning nearly as much as Darryl did. They wouldn't lose so much if Sharon weren't moving from an S filing status—single—and Darryl weren't switching from HH—head of household. The problem was that they were now stuck in what was called MFJ—married, filing jointly. And so on.

What Sharon perceived, and what McIntosh appreciated, was that there was a greater problem behind such arcana: the federal tax code was restricting her freedom. In the same letter that described her tax situation, she wrote that it seemed inappropriate that Washington should even ask that she and Darryl supply information about their relationship. "Employers, bankers, realtors, and creditors are forbidden by law to ask these questions. The same should apply to the government."

Everyone involved understood that this was, in its way, a very American statement. Sharon was really saying what many citizens feel—that they pride themselves on marriages. That they are especially proud that they have the freedom to construct these marriages themselves. That they build their marriages, in privacy, like houses, taking pleasure in that construction, puttering endlessly, making little changes here and there, evaluating choices. What other country has room to glorify, or at least tolerate, as many celebrations of marriage as the Las Vegas elopement, the engraved invitation, evening black tie at morning weddings, and same-sex parenting?

The McIntosh staff realized that the marriage penalty cut at that autonomy, corseting women. It forced on them a rigid ultimatum: marry or work. Families could avoid the marriage penalty, but only if the second earner, usually a woman, did not work, or worked just a little. This left women with a terribly confining choice, the choice between living as *Ozzie and Harriet* or as *Murphy Brown.*

Nor was that choice easy to escape. It occurred at the top end of the income scale. A New York City attorney told of couples who went through church ceremonies for their families but never married legally, so that they could avoid the penalty. And it confronted poor families, discouraging the jobless and lower earners. The American Institute of Certified Public Accountants sifted through the federal tax code to find which sections generated a marriage penalty. A full sixty-six parts of the code, from low-income housing credits and the child tax credit to adoption expenses and the alternative minimum tax, punished married pairs that worked.

Most American families didn't analyze their tax troubles to this degree. They knew, instinctively, that their tax burden was high. Working couples knew that it was higher than it had been when they were single, or at least that they thought about taxes more than they had then. And they knew that somehow the numbers were more logical when the wife didn't work. A full twenty-five million couples, mostly couples with just one earner, actually enjoyed a "marriage bonus"—paying less tax on their income than they would on the same income if they were single. But they enjoyed that "bonus" at a cost—the cost of forgoing the opportunity for the second adult in the household to earn a significant income. Many families blamed the change on recessions, the payroll tax, or just plain old "middle-class squeeze." Some accepted it as part of the sacrifice they made to marry. The new cost seemed part of the bargain they struck with the phrase "for richer or poorer."

In the 1990s, though, the consequences of all this policy had become more and more visible. When one partner earned much more than the other, or the second partner did not work at all, there was no penalty. When both partners in a marriage earn the same, or about the same, there was a marriage penalty. In practical terms this means that women who built careers for themselves, poor or rich, paid higher taxes than women who didn't. Undereducated wives who chose to educate themselves, in the very sense the welfare reforms encouraged, subjected themselves to the most wicked marriage penalty of all.

McIntosh knew that recent changes in the federal code had made the marriage penalty even worse. President Bush's rate hike raised the penalty. President Clinton and Congress's decision to raise rates again ratcheted up the marriage penalty. In the same years, all of Washington, left and right, showed a penchant for creating small, targeted tax breaks at the bottom of the income scale. Each of these ostensibly family-friendly measures also worsened the marriage penalty.

McIntosh raised all this in a September 1997 speech to the Christian Coalition, describing how the Republicans' child credit, the centerpiece of the Contract with America, actually contributed to the marriage penalty. "Under the budget we passed," he explained to the credit's backers, "many families only receive a portion of the $500 tax child credit because they are married and earn too much money." The reason for this was that when couples married, their combined incomes pushed them right out of the income range eligible for the sort of family breaks they now needed the most.

Losing $3,701

Around the time that McIntosh started getting excited about solving the marriage-penalty problem, a Washington research group, the Polling Company, did a study for Republicans. It found that 77 percent of Americans favored getting rid of the penalty, 56 percent strongly so. And, in the same months, the Congressional Budget Office published the first thorough study on the marriage penalty to appear in years. The study included an example of a very wealthy couple, a pair earning $300,000 each. They paid a marriage penalty of $16,000. It looked at a middle-income couple, earning $37,500 each, finding that the couple paid $1,391 more in tax than they would have had they remained single. And it demonstrated the scope of the marriage penalty on the poor, a couple who had two children and who earned only $11,000 each. That couple paid an extra $3,701 in taxes because of their marital status.

Faced with these numbers, McIntosh and others in Washington had to stop and wonder. This was, after all, the 1990s, a time when "family preservation" was a political buzzword and just about every political force in Washington was pushing to help poorer families stay together. How was it that the federal tax code worked so hard to keep those families apart? Then there was a more fundamental question: why did America, the nation whose women had shown the world that wives can work, still penalize those women for doing exactly that?

Uncle Sam's Dowry

To appreciate the challenge the McIntosh team faced in engineering away the marriage penalty for the family, it helps to understand that the penalty was itself a result of earlier efforts at profamily engineering. Some of those first steps came in the late 1940s, the beginning of the baby boom and an era far more uniformly family-oriented than any we could envision today. The nation had just come out of a long period of deficit—in this instance, the deficit caused by World War II. There was no "married, filing jointly" status as there is today. Individuals, even husbands whose wives did not work, filed as though they were single. Taxes were very high, crossing, for better earners, into the 70 percent range.

In some states, though, married couples enjoyed some relief from this. They were allowed to split their incomes and be taxed on their half—even if one partner, the man, had earned all the income. The states that had these rules— California, Louisiana, Texas—had them because of obscure features in their legal systems, features that stemmed in some cases from Napoleonic law. These legal details were of interest to few people beyond tax lawyers. What mattered was that with federal rates as high as they were, income splitting made these states attractive. Instead of facing a 77 percent rate on the last dollar he earned, a man could enjoy a much lower rate if he allocated half the income, on paper, to his wife. The savings were so substantial that between 1939 and 1948 five states and Hawaii actually switched to community property arrangements. When in 1941 a congressman proposed barring the states from doing this, he met a storm of protest, couched, whenever the protestors could manage it, in indignant promarriage, profamily language. Critics charged that his plan was "a tax on morality" and would generate divorce. As Barber Conable, the World Bank chairman and congressman was to say later, in a different context, "Hell hath no greater fury than a vested interest masquerading as a moral principle."

War's end brought change: suddenly lawmakers were confronted with a surprise budget surplus, the peace dividend. Rather like the Republicans today, the Republicans who ran the House in that era talked about using the surplus for families. Wealthy easterners who didn't live in the states with income splitting were envious of those who did. Instead of banning income splitting, Congress decided it would make this tax advantage available to all Americans, throughout the land. Each would pay the tax rate that applied to their half of the money—a much lower rate than one earner would have paid alone on that income. To arrange for couples to enjoy this break, Congress created the MFJ status—"married, filing jointly."

MFJ was indeed quite a gift—one observer, an economist at General Motors named Ludwig S. Hellborn, called it "Uncle Sam's dowry." And it was a dowry for the mothers who would give the country the baby boom. Demographer Leslie Whittington has argued that the favorable tax situation for married couples actually boosted the birthrate. She uncovered what she called a "robust" relationship between fertility and the personal income tax exemption.

The Wife as Tax Advantage

The men of that period savored their marital tax advantage with a proprietary glee that today seems dated, if not offputting. Philip Stern, the author of a book on the numerous tax loopholes that were the rule in the postwar period, gave as good a sample of the mood as any in his description of Jeremy Hornblower, a hypothetical young bridegroom. "It is his wedding day: at noon he is to become conjugally joined with a delectable southern maiden, Sue Alice Beauregard. . . . At 12:17 the minister ties the knot, and at that instant Jeremy's annual tax bill drops." Stern even calculated the amount Jeremy would have to keep in a bank to get the same savings he got by merely being married. "[B]asking on the beach at Waikiki, our honeymooning bridegroom can take a satisfied glance at that $17,742 asset lying by his side." Stern also made note of the hefty marriage penalty that existed in those years as well, saying of this object-wife that "if she wishes to keep her cash value at a maximum, she must at all costs avoid remunerative activity."

Soon, though, this "profamily" work did exactly what it would do today—provoke the ire of single people. Single men working beside their colleagues in offices and factories discovered that the fellow in the next office paid substantially lower taxes—just because he was married. The singles movement had a breathless, ebullient spokesperson, the same lonely tax warrior who had led the aborted fight against withholding: Vivien Kellems. Miss Kellems, herself single, established the War Widows of America to lobby against the singles penalty. In her book, *Toil, Taxes and Trouble,* Kellems laid out her argument against the 1948 law. "I'm quite sure that if Congress had come out honestly and proposed a tax upon single people, just because they are single, that law could never have been passed, but as usual, a slick trick was slipped into a tax law and when the Federal Community Tax Law was passed, it automatically slapped a tax upon millions of people just because they were not married.

"Considering the fact that there are many, many more women than men in our country and that due to the sheer preponderance of numbers, these women can never be married, is it fair to pile an additional tax on them for a condition which they cannot help and which 99 and 44/100 percent would change if they could? And what about the widows with children?"

Kellems got farther in her fight against the singles penalty than she had with her withholding struggle. As tax scholar Michael Graetz reports, actress Gloria Swanson rallied to Miss Kellems's side, testifying before Congress that, although she had been married numerous times, she had spent more time single and knew that single people needed more support from the tax code. Protestors by the thousands mailed tea bags to the Ways and Means chairman, Wilbur Mills. Among Kellems's allies was an (unmarried) congressman named Ed Koch, who later became New York City's mayor. Eventually, lawmakers caved, rewriting the law to cap the advantage traditional married couples had over everyone else. For war widows they established the category "head of household," which lessened the advantage of marriage. Later they helped singles by adjusting the tax tables to limit the disparity between the rates for single filers and couples.

Galbraith's Campaign

But these were years in which American society was seeing big changes. The nation was feeling a strong need to fight for social justice. It wanted to do something else for the family, specifically, the poor family: tax the rich. The tax device used to implement that desire is called progressivity. In a progressive structure, rates rise as earnings go up. Although progressivity had been around since the beginning of the income tax, it was only in the 1950s and 1960s that the middle class embraced the idea as socially necessary. The year 1958 saw the publication of John Kenneth Galbraith's *The Affluent Society,* in which the economist chided upper-middle-class America for its prosperous complacency. Galbraith worried about the "capacity for not seeing what we do not wish to see." He said that Americans' obliviousness "enables us to travel in comfort by Harlem and into the lush precincts of midtown Manhattan." Galbraith wrote about a New Class, by which he meant college professors, attorneys, and the white-collar upper crust generally, who oughtn't mind paying extra taxes because they cared only about prestige anyway. Galbraith even berated his New Class for their occasional complaint about taxes: "These are people who, by their own claim except when they are talking about income taxes, are not primarily motivated by money." Galbraith's book was an instant classic. It was the landmark authority on what was then known as the "new economics of abundance."

The new head-of-household category was born of the same progressive spirit. Long after the war widows' problems faded, socially minded thinkers pushed to retain the head of household status because it gave single parents some of the tax advantages of being married. In the very years that the Department of Health, Education and Welfare was working hard to build supports for single mothers into Aid for Families with Dependent Children, the tax experts at the Treasury Department were working to build parallel supports for single-parent families into the tax code. Soon head-of-household filers had many of the advantages of being married—without being married. Eventually the tax laws even allowed married couples to opt for the tax advantages of unmarried status without getting an official divorce or separation. (This category bore the quaint name "married, but unmarried for tax purposes.") The change gave a financial advantage to working parents who lived apart from a spouse without having officially separated. But it hardly made marriage more attractive.

A Burden for Women

In these years, too, a far more important shift was taking place. Betty Friedan wrote *The Feminine Mystique*. Women were going to work. In the 1950s only one in four wives worked outside the home. By 1995 three quarters of all couples with a working husband also had a working wife.

The result was something no one had predicted. When women went to work, they drove household income up into tax brackets that Congress—and, one may presume, John Kenneth Galbraith—had never envisioned for them. This was so for a simple reason. Under a progressive system, not all income was taxed at the same rate. The additional money a family earned made it look like a wealthier household, one that, under the system, was taxed at the higher rate.

This meant that these new workers, usually unskilled women, were actually paying taxes at higher rates than their husbands did, even when they earned less money. In the language of tax writers, this problem had a specific name—"second-earner bias."

If the journalists of the period had named it, they could have called it "the women's rate," or more accurately, the "successful wives' rate." Most journalists, though, didn't name it, and most Americans never analyzed their financial situation. They only knew that they were beginning to suffer a terrible sort of bracket creep, not the kind caused by inflation but what might be called marital bracket creep. The only families who were exempt from this were traditional families. Because of a relatively generous standard deduction and other breaks, families with stay-at-home moms still enjoyed a marriage bonus.

It is a testimony to the desire of women to return to work, and of their spouses' support for that desire, that they actually did so in the face of this challenge. Marital bracket creep was particularly hard on women who were considering going back to work after a hiatus like child rearing. That is because these women often earned little. The main effect of their decision, therefore, was not to enrich the family but merely to move the family into a higher bracket. Although people did not verbalize this situation, they certainly verbalized its result. How many American women have said, or heard their mothers say, "When I first started work my salary was just enough to pay the baby-sitter"?

The budgeteers in Washington saw the situation entirely differently. They treated the revenues from working wives' wages the same way they treated any other new revenue streams—as found money. What had started out as a tax cut in the 1940s was now a source of cash for the most expensive American government in peacetime history. Lawmakers were reluctant to give up their billions.

This reluctance explains an anomaly that still confronts every taxpayer today. It is that oddball tax status known as MFS, or married, filing separately. MFS sounds intriguing, and plenty of people, including many marriage-penalty victims, run the numbers on MFS to see if they can regain the tax advantage they had as singles. But various Congresses and a number of presidents have ensured that taxpayers would not be able to escape to lower rates via this door. They did this by attaching all sorts of special penalties to the MFS category. The beleaguered MFS filer cannot claim the Earned Income Credit. He cannot take a standard deduction if his spouse itemizes, and he may not claim two 1990s breaks, the Hope Scholarship or the lifetime earning credit. He may exclude only $250,000 of the profit he makes on the sale of his house, instead of the $500,000 allowed the privileged MFJ's. MFS is, in short, a sham. The only way to get out of the marriage penalty is to pretend to separate, to separate (married, but unmarried for tax purposes), or to divorce (single or head of houschold).

Divorce for Fun and Profit

The very first "modern" marriage-penalty protest was mounted by a working Maryland couple named David and Angela Boyter. In December of 1975 the Boyters traveled to Haiti for a winter vacation. While they were there, they obtained a divorce, a change that meant they could claim single status on the 1975 return. Back in Maryland in January, they remarried. Come that December, the Boyters traveled to the Caribbean again. This time their destination was the Dominican Republic. There they got divorced again. Then they returned to the United States and remarried. By filing as singles, the couple saved $3,000 a year in taxes. At the time, as Angela Boyter noted publicly, that was more than enough to pay for the Caribbean vacation. So proud were the pair of their plan that they even published a pamphlet about it: *Divorce for Fun and Profit.*

Divorce for Fun and Profit did not go over well in sober American courts. A divorce for tax purposes, the judges said, was not divorce. It was a "sham transaction." Even as they unfurled their ruling against the Boyters, though, the judges stopped to note their understanding of the Boyters' dilemma: "Undoubtedly, all this confusion is a bit bewildering to the average citizen, who may assume that simple justice and administrative convenience would be best served by taxing income to the individual who earns it," commented the court, adding resignedly that "nevertheless, Congress through the years responded to a variety of problems on an ad hoc basis and we now have still another problem, the 'marriage penalty.'" In the 1980s Congress seemed, at least for a while, to forsake that ad hoc basis with marriage-penalty relief it provided in the 1981 law and the lower overall rates of 1986. But by the 1990s things had worsened. One reason was that women were doing very well. As the wage gap narrowed, they started to earn as much as their husbands. And couples in which two earners each made about the same paid the highest marriage penalties of all.

The 1990s also brought new marriage penalties for lower earners. That is because all the targeted breaks that were popular in the era were breaks that were phased out. And any couple whose joint income brought them to the phase-out level suffered a wicked marriage penalty. These were the problems that concerned McIntosh. One of the worst of these, the one that created the shocking losses for poor people, was the mischievous Earned Income Credit, the tax rebate designed to keep low earners in the work force.

Every tax season tax preparers saw a dramatic illustration of the result of the EIC. A family arrived at a tax-preparation office together, two parents with as many as three or four children. But rather than claim together, the parents split up, each one taking at least one child and going to two different tax preparers. Each one then filed his return as head of household. If the couple was married and lived together, they had to lie about their lives. But if they had never married, there was no problem at all.

A Tectonic Clash

The truth was that what seemed a small and technical problem, the marriage penalty, was really something much bigger, a tectonic clash of two social goals of the postwar period. The first, equality for the poor, gave the nation progressive tax schedules and expensive government. The second, equality for women, gave the nation working wives. Punishing the "rich" turned out to mean punishing another group the country perceives to be vulnerable—women beginning a career. Women's groups, who might have seemed the natural candidates for taking up the marriage penalty, were reluctant to criticize, let alone attack, an icon like progressivity. They focused on helping very poor families and single mothers and left middle-class married couples to fend for themselves. They publicized the "wage gap"—the discrepancy between women's and men's earnings. But they ignored the tax gap, the difference between wives' tax rates and their husbands'.

Through the 1980s the battle was between two visions of the needs of the family. The Democrats, including the women among them, focused on aiding the poor family, a group in which they included single parents, by fighting for progressivity and the revenues it could generate. The Republicans focused on helping the family by helping individuals, married or not, who aspired to move up the income scale. Their aim was reducing progressivity. As a result the 1980s fights—in which McIntosh participated as an assistant to President Reagan for domestic policy—were not so much about the marriage penalty, although there was an item in the Economic Recovery Tax Act that alleviated the marriage penalty for some people. They were about overall rates. The Tax Reform Act of 1986 curtailed progressivity, which lowered tax punishments overall, including marriage penalties. But at least the parameters were on the table. Or so McIntosh thought.

The Social Conservatives

In the 1990s a third force emerged in the marriage-penalty wars: the social conservatives. The Christian Coalition and other groups on the religious right wanted to promote marriage—especially traditional marriage. Their argument was an important one: that marriage had economic value. It protected, it shielded, it did the work of a thousand public programs. Even after the nation's landmark welfare reform shifted many Americans from the welfare rolls into the workforce, the data were stark. Bureau of Labor Statistics data from January 1998 show that the category "women who maintain families"—essentially, single women—had unemployment of 7.6 percent. This compared with 3.1 percent for married women with a spouse and 2.6 percent for married men with spouse present.

The social conservatives had a powerful reason for focusing on the marriage penalty. They noted that American society had long valued office and factory work enough to give them all sorts of tax favors. But "home work" had won few tax advantages. They acknowledged that there was a "marriage bonus" in tax terms for the single-earner couple. But they said that wasn't nearly enough. Most of the major social legislation in the tax code aimed to shore up single-parent families and often gave these families tax breaks that were not available to MFJ couples. The social conservatives noted that the standard deduction, once a central support of the MFJ crowd, had not been increased over the years to keep pace with inflation.

And they worked on developing the argument that families were an important economic unit, one that needed more significant support. Allan Carlson, editor of the conservative *Family in America,* summed up this view: "We need to recognize that there are two economies that always exist: the market economy, where exchanges take place through the medium of official tender and where competition and the quest for efficiency drive decisions; and the home economy, where exchanges occur through the altruistic blending of wealth and services among family members, usually independent of monetary calculation." The explicit aim here was to put through a tax policy that promoted the sort of family-as-nest life the nation lived in the 1950s—the return to *Ozzie and Harriet.*

Everyone, including the Democrats on the other side of the aisle, knew this was an important addition to the discussion, and that it brought out some of what had been wrong with tax and welfare policy in recent decades. They also knew that voters responded powerfully to the argument that tax law and social policy were hurting the family. They knew this was part of the reason for the success of conservative talk radio. Dr. James Dobson, the founder of *Focus on Family,* a radio show that aired daily on more than 2,900 stations across the country, often talked about tax problems. Many Republicans thought they could unite the goals of the Dr. Dobsons of the world with their free-market, Reaganite goals of cutting marginal tax rates. That was what the Contract with America had tried to do. Certainly, that was McIntosh's hope.

But anyone who ran the numbers, and many people eventually did, found there was a problem. You could have progressivity, you could have low rates for the second earner, and you could have a tax arrangement that buttressed the traditional family. But you could not have all three. When you treated married women who worked as individuals, you gave them and their husbands a tax advantage over traditional couples—at least as long as there was progressivity. And when you buttressed the tax supports for married couples with a stay-at-home wife while retaining progressivity, you punished couples with working wives.

Of course, when you reduced progressivity, middle-class traditional families did better, and so did middle-class families with two earners. This had been the achievement of McIntosh's forerunners in the Republican party, accomplished with support of a Democratic Congress. Now, in the 1990s, reducing progressivity would also cut back the wicked marriage penalty on the crowd collecting the Earned Income Credit. But President Clinton and most Democrats were opposed to reducing progressivity, basically because they didn't want to reward wealthy families too much. The social conservatives in the party didn't care about ending progressivity; they wanted programs to help the traditional family. By default, the mid-1990s had become an era of loophole writing, and cutting back progressivity was the possibility that seemed the furthest away of all.

The Effort Founders

McIntosh was among those slowed by this trouble, both personally and politically. In the fall of 1997, his wife, Ruthie, gave birth to their first baby, a girl they named Ellie, and decided to stay home with the child. At winter conferences in Washington he laid out his plan, noting that the Christian Coalition and the Catholics backed him, that he had their endorsement right on his Web site.

But then came the criticism. Some of the social conservatives started to point out that his plan, allowing couples to choose between MFJ, HH, and S, took away some of the tax advantages enjoyed by many traditional families. Maggie Gallagher, a national newspaper columnist and a contemporary of McIntosh's at Yale, criticized the McIntosh plan for sending mothers out into the workplace. In February McIntosh attended a meeting at the Senate's Dirksen Office Building where representatives of the Howard Center for the Family, Religion, & Society and the Institute for American Values, two socially conservative think tanks, assailed his project. McIntosh stood his ground but had to leave early, as it happened, to attend a floor vote on renaming National Airport after his hero, Ronald Reagan. As soon as McIntosh left the room, the think tank people started talking about how important it was to write law that was *really* promarriage.

Within a week their criticism had also showed up in the *Weekly Standard,* an influential magazine that spoke for the new 1990s conservatism. The article attacked McIntosh and his cosponsor, Jerry Weller of Illinois, for promoting "individualization of the tax code." The authors, Allan Carlson and David Blankenhorn, wrote that Congress must reject the McIntosh proposal, which, they charged, would yield a "homemaker penalty." They backed a rule that would allow married couples to split their income, even if all of it was earned by just one partner, and file at lower rates.

Lauch Faircloth of North Carolina, a Republican, was sponsoring income-splitting legislation. Connie Mack, a Republican from Florida who sat on the Finance Committee and was senior to McIntosh, was also a sponsor. Their plan also at first sounded good to McIntosh, who was looking for resolution. But it had the effect of giving an additional bonus to people who already enjoyed the most favorable of the four tax statuses—traditional families with one main earner.

More important, it would also favor all married couples over singles. It would allow anyone who was married, traditional or two-earner, to escape the high marginal rates of the income tax. This meant there would be a kind of apartheid of tax regimes. Married couples would be in the less progressive regime. But singles would be stuck with the old high rates.

McIntosh knew that singles had their lobbies too, including the well-organized gay lobby. The last thing McIntosh wanted was to be charged with discrimination, or to be the sponsor of a piece of legislation that became a cause célèbre. Others recognized this problem as well. "Even if changes left their taxes unaffected," the Congressional Budget Office had warned a year earlier, "single filers might object that lowering the taxes of married couples would leave singles worse off in relative terms, again paying higher taxes because they are single than they would if they were married."

The final blow was that income splitting was expensive, which frightened the fiscal conservatives among the Republicans. They didn't want to give the president the high ground and the chance to present them as big spenders. The mere introduction of the Faircloth bill gave the administration all the opening it needed to take up—and dismiss—the project. "The marriage penalty is a problem," secretary of the Treasury Robert Rubin said on the TV show *Evans & Novak* on March 21. "And we are sympathetic to the problem. But the problem is that if we fix that and preserve the marriage bonus, and as you know a lot of people get a marriage bonus, [it] would cost us something like thirty billion dollars a year, [and] over a five-year period, one hundred fifty billion." Rubin echoed the president's State of the Union message of that year, in which the president had spoken about families by talking about reforming Social Security. "It is our view," Rubin said as he summed up his thoughts, "that that issue should not be addressed until Social Security has been addressed."

McIntosh, one of the more formidable of the younger

lawmakers, did not give up easily. Somehow, there had to be an affordable way to help the family that did not stir the ire of the Christian right and did not alienate free marketeers. But soon the marriage penalty, which so many had hoped would become the tax issue of 1998, seemed to go on hold, to the chagrin of all the staffers who had worked so hard on the topic crunching numbers and tracking down couples like Sharon and Darryl.

As 1998 drew to a close and elections neared, the failing marriage penalty legislation came to symbolize the greater failure of the Republican party to unify on important issues, and the failure of the Democrats to play a meaningful role in addressing Americans' tax troubles. Cutting rates overall for every kind of household would have helped things, but lawmakers in both parties had refused to think on such a scale, refused to give up their tinkering. With their focus on "marriage," Republicans had wasted a year, a year in which they might have pushed for broad tax reform. (One Republican aide described the marriage penalty episode as "letting the tail of social conservatism wag the dog of economic policy.") As for the Democrats, they too had done damage. With their focus on tax breaks for the poor— expansions of the Earned Income Credit for example—they had inadvertently hurt the poor, at a cost to their middle- and upper-middle-class constituents.

Over and over again, the politicians pondered their problem. Everyone involved wanted to help the American family through specific tax relief. They knew they could use the tax code to engineer that change, if only they worked hard enough, and if only they could agree on who that family ought to be.

5

YOUR HOUSE

AMERICANS WHO ARE BUYING THEIR FIRST HOME TEND TO feel a little righteous. They take this enormous step with the conviction of people who know that virtue is on their side. Their parents taught them that there is a merit, a merit of a very grown-up nature, to being "house poor." They've been told a thousand times that it is time to "stop throwing away money on rent." Now they are stopping.

Indeed, there's a quiet little monologue that people speak to themselves when they make their big purchase. It runs something like this: Here I come, responsibility. Here I come, lawn work. I'm married now, we may say. I am committed, and I am going to prove it by yoking myself into thirty years of servitude to a bank.

As with many of life's sacrifices, there's a consolation here. It is the consolation of taxpayers who, finally, after years of working, are getting a crack at turning the system to their advantage through the home-mortgage deduction. This, they say to themselves, is the thing the greedy hand allows me—the big thing that I get. And it is something I need right now. To a pair riding the seas of the payroll tax, the income tax, and the marriage penalty, the home-mortgage deduction looms like an island. The deductibility of real estate is the added gift, the spring of clear water on that island.

Recently the magazine *Smart Money* broke out the details of this advantage for readers. A taxpayer making a $1,200 mortgage payment every month can deduct about $1,080 of that at the beginning of his loan, when most of the monthly bill is still interest. That cuts his taxable income by something like $13,000 a year. If you're in the 28 percent bracket that the magazine studied, you save about $300 a month.

Citizens tend to hear the word *savings* and jump. Three hundred dollars a month, they say to themselves. Sign me up! We are going to have a kitchen with hardwood floors, we tell ourselves, and we are going to personally seed that lawn. And at the same time, we are going to get our turn to enjoy the home deduction, the biggest tax boondoggle in modern America. One of the best things about the boondoggle is that it is a deduction, not a credit. It doesn't phase out with higher earnings, like so many of the new credits Congress has built in. In fact, it gets more powerful when you earn more. The home-mortgage deduction saves a person with the top tax rate of 50 percent a whole lot more than it saves a person with a 20 percent rate.

A Municipal Bond You Can Sleep In

There's added satisfaction in the thought that we are going to get to *use* our tax deduction while we receive it. A house is a much more handy thing to have than a piece of paper that says you own a tax-exempt security or a share in an oil-well project, to name two other shelters. Tom Ochsen-schlager, a partner in the accounting firm Grant, Thornton, calls a home with a mortgage "a municipal bond you can sleep in."

Finally, there's the comfort of numbers. Somehow, most Americans have gained the impression "that everyone takes the home-mortgage deduction." Certainly, many congress-people do: indeed, they claim it twice, once for their Washington house and once for the house they maintain back home in their district. The papers reported the Clintons claimed one of $3,263 in 1996 because they paid half the costs of the home of Dorothy Rodham, Mrs. Clinton's mother. This comfort is something of an illusion: the home owners who don't take the deduction outnumber those who do. Still, we tend to ignore that fact and concentrate on our fellow deduc-tors. Hey, Americans say to themselves as they sign a thou-sand dotted lines, 29.5 million taxpayers can't be wrong.

A Better Investment

Or can they? The home-mortgage deduction is indeed a wonderful thing. But only in the context of Americans' lives as they live them now. Look outside that to other contexts— say, the context of another, less taxed life—and the home-mortgage deduction starts to look more like an obligation than an oasis.

This becomes clear if you run another set of numbers. Take a woman who had $100,000 in the fall of 1993 and used that money as a down payment on a $200,000 house. She got the house, and she got to pay "rent" on top of that— her monthly mortgage. Five years later, she is still paying the bank its money. But the economy is bouncing along, the neighborhood has improved, and today her home value is $300,000 or more. She doubled her original $100,000.

But say that, instead, she didn't buy the house. She put that $100,000 in PIMco Growth Fund A, a garden-variety mutual fund favored by families for college saving. PIMco Growth Fund A went up an average of 20 percent *a year* in the same period, which means it did more than double. If she had put her principal in the market those five years and postponed the house, she would be able to buy a bigger house now. Home values in most areas have not kept up with the stock market. Capital-gains rates are even coming down, so that making money off that money is easier. Some investors just put their savings in an IRA or a 401(k) and watch these better profits grow untaxed.

For some people, houses are a big bargain. Those are people with cash to spare, people who can ride the rates. That is to say, they take a loan for their house at 7 percent, a loan that frequently boasts the bonus of being guaranteed by federal insurance. This leaves spare cash to play the market and earn 8, 10, or 20 percent. They make 1, 3, or even 13 percent—not a bad arrangement.

But many people have little or no cash left over to play the market after fulfilling their house wishes. They do get tens of thousands or even more in "tax savings" from the mortgage-interest deduction and its sister, the property-tax deduction. But they often need that money to put central air into the money pit, the house. They may console themselves by fixing their eyes on the pot of gold at the end of the rainbow. Thirty years down the road, if the home value rises, and if Congress doesn't change the laws, they can reap the profits on the sale of their house *untaxed.* Another unique advantage! But those, given the fickle nature of markets and politicians, are two very big ifs. And for now these people are stuck, enjoying their central air, serving the mortgage, and serving the house. They don't call it "house poor" for nothing.

None of this, of course, is laid out for citizens by the lawmakers, the banks, the real estate people. They defend the home-mortgage deduction as if it were a baby's cradle. They focus on the "tax savings," however secondary those savings are. Lawmakers, you have to remember, have an interest to defend here, a very personal interest: most of them are stuck maintaining homes in their constituencies. Banks and real estate people have even more obvious reasons to fight against sweeping changes that would eliminate the break. Every time the question of tax reform raises its head in Washington, the Realtors™, a mighty lobby so pretentious that it insists the little trademark symbol accompany every print mention of its name, go out in numbers to convince everyone that the sky will fall on American families if the advantage disappears.

Politics, Not Families

The story of how the home-mortgage deduction came to play such a central role in our lives is a story of politics, not benefits for families. From the very beginning of time—in this case the Tariff Act of 1913, which created the income tax—people have been allowed to deduct interest expenses. Until 1986, as many adults still recall, those "interest expenses" included credit card debt. The 1986 law ended the credit card break, which made the house deduction look all the more precious. By now anyone who plans to criticize the home-mortgage deduction must arm for lobbying Armageddon. In 1995, when talk of a flat tax was heard across the nation, the real estate lobby blanketed the nation with fear-mongering pamphlets warning of a collapse in home values should a flat tax come.

So how has the home-mortgage deduction come to be the national Holy Grail? The first answer is that it is powerful because it is a *relative* advantage among a sea of disadvantages that dominate our tax culture. In the context of progressive income tax rates and all the tax credits that are available to families only as long as they stay in certain income brackets, the home-mortgage deduction is one of the few remaining tax advantages that becomes even stronger the more Americans earn. The advantage to a family that earns $50,000 a year and puts 5 percent down on a home is nothing special. But families who earn more—even if that "more" just happened because they got married and now pay the marriage penalty—need it a lot. When you are paying $25,000 a year in federal taxes, the kind of tax bill that confronted a single filer with no house and taxable income of $100,000 in 1997, that little nest and its deduction start to look very tempting. In many states, someone in the 39.6 percent bracket for the income tax, the top rate, faces an effective 50 percent tax rate. So getting a tax deduction at that level is getting a tax deduction worth 50¢ for every dollar. Presidents Bush and Clinton and succeeding Congresses sweetened the home-mortgage breaks by raising tax rates.

Even better, home owners can use their home ownership to get tax breaks on borrowing that has nothing to do with their house, as long as they and a bank agree to call their borrowing a home equity loan. If you buy a car, for example, with home-equity loan money, you can deduct the borrowing costs of that car. You don't even have to prove you actually spent the money on lumber you didn't need at the Home Depot or the services of a local contractor. You can just borrow the "house" money, up to $100,000 of it, and buy the car. Many a leather-seated Volvo or Chrysler van is purchased this way. If you're going to own the home anyway, this is sheer gravy.

Then there is the powerful lesson of our parents. If you're thirty-five now, there's a good chance your parents bought their first home for $25,000 in 1962 and paid 5 percent interest on their thirty-year fixed mortgage. Then came inflation, a time when it was very good to be a borrower. In those days people didn't have adjustable-rate mortgages that passed along the economy's pain. Their loan was secured at a fixed interest rate. Every time our parents had to make a payment, the money they had to pay was worth less to them. And when time came to sell—in the 1980s, say—that house sold for up to ten or even twenty times its old price. Best of all, many of our parents didn't pay capital-gains taxes on a good share of their profit—they were allowed to defer those gains into eternity as they bought another, bigger house. Making the sacrifice to be house poor certainly paid off for them.

Different from Our Parents

But that doesn't mean it will pay off for younger Americans. For one, markets are freer, technology is stronger, and so there are other places to invest our money. For another thing, we haven't had the scale of inflation our parents faced for years, and at this writing, we don't look likely to have it in the future. So being a borrower is not such a good idea. Inflation, indeed, was what helped our parents' houses appreciate so wildly in the first place. After the United States went off the gold-exchange standard in the early 1970s, there was a flight to value—to oil, for one thing, as we recall from the gas-station lines, and to real estate, for another. We, by contrast, are not necessarily likely to see our homes quintuple in value over thirty years. But the parental model is hard to shake.

Then there is the political risk. For years politicians gave families a break on the sale of their homes. They didn't have to pay capital-gains tax on the increased value of the house at the time they sold it. Anyone, from your mother to Donald Trump, could use this advantage.

But the rules that applied to the break were numerous. You had to buy another house within a couple of years or you didn't get the break. And that house had to be as valuable as, or more valuable than, your previous house. If you were downsizing, say, buying a condo, you were stuck paying capital gains. The only way to limit that punishment was to show you'd put more into the house than the original purchase price. This led people to pour enormous amounts of energy into improving their homes. In the years they owned the home, they spent thousands improving it—because they liked to improve, but also because documented improvement stepped up the official basis of what they have spent on real estate and reduced their "profit" at the time of sale. This was good for photocopy shops, where the home owners copied religiously to prepare their tax records. It was good for Wal-Mart and Home Depot stock-holders. But was it really what everyone wanted to be doing?

Then, in 1997, the politicians changed the game. Now you pay no capital gains up to a certain amount of your profit on your house, even if you don't buy another. But here again, there are pitfalls: for married individuals that amount is their first $500,000 in profit; for singles it is only $250,000. You have to own the house for a certain time. If you rent a second home out for more than fourteen days, you run into snags—the revenue becomes taxable. And so on.

A House of Cards

The message here is not that the current rules are bad. Right now they are pretty good. It is that they change. In fact Congress changes the tax rules on houses nearly as frequently as many Americans change houses. When you buy a house, you lock yourself in to servitude to a political lobby: the home-mortgage lobby. Your home-mortgage benefit is a house of cards, which can collapse with a mere flick of the wrist from the greedy hand.

At this point you may be half convinced of the mortgage deduction's limits. But, one might ask, what about this mighty edifice of government subsidy, $50 billion worth in 1996, that the home mortgage represents? What about the fact that government, in some way or other, insures more than 40 percent of homes right now? Won't that whole edifice come tumbling down, and my property values with it, should we fiddle with the home-mortgage deduction? I don't like being vulnerable, you may say. But at this point, I'm not an objective observer. I'm a person with too much to lose.

One answer, and an important one, is that a simpler tax structure with lower rates and no home-mortgage deduction will indeed change things. One thing it will change is our dependence on Washington home lobbyists. Another thing it is very likely to change is interest rates. In fact, a simpler regime with no mortgage deduction is very likely to bring interest rates *down*. That's because interest rates are prices like any other. And prices are set at what people can pay—"what the traffic will bear," to use the term favored by one of our nation's best Treasury secretaries, the late Andrew Mellon. When tax breaks are available, people are willing to pay a higher price for something. They will earn a lower return or pay a higher interest rate to get them.

If this sounds too technical, just consider the difference between interest rates on municipal bonds, which are tax-exempt, and regular bonds from the federal government, which aren't. In the 1990s, people were willing to take a return of a percentage point or lower on a municipal bond just to get the tax break. We're also willing to pay more on home loans for the same reason.

If the tax advantage disappears, the current interest rates for mortgages are going to start to look expensive. Lenders are going to have to work harder to get us to borrow their money or as much of it. So interest rates will come down. The Tax Foundation, an independent group that crunches numbers on state and federal finance, estimates that interest rates generally would come down enough to save families many thousands each year.

Another point is that in a system where real estate doesn't enjoy a huge advantage over other investments, our economy would grow more efficiently overall. The 1980s roller coaster of commercial real estate was a perfect example. In the early 1980s lawmakers gave powerful tax advantages to mall building. Thousands of tax-generated strip malls duly rose across the land—far more than even shopping-happy America could use. When that tax advantage disappeared, the malls still needed customers. But they didn't have enough, and without a tax advantage, they didn't have enough investors. The nation had to pay hundreds of billions for the whole mess when the savings-and-loan crisis erupted. S & L's downfall widened the ensuing recession.

The upside of this is that when the market isn't distorted, to use the economists' term, the better investments do better. The money goes somewhere because there is money to be made there, not just because it is federally insured or offers a tax advantage. Your Intel or your PIMco growth fund, for that matter, will do better, because the market will be able to treat real estate as what it really is: housing stock, not a tax game.

So the next time you build a sunroom instead of buying a mutual fund, you can say several things to yourself. One is that you are getting a nicer house. Another is that you are making a good investment, given your circumstances. But it may not necessarily be the best of investments, the one that could earn you the most in the best of all possible worlds. A house is a home, but it is also a trap.

6

YOUR BABY

IN THE SPRING OF 1998 DISNEY ANNOUNCED THE RELEASE of the movie *Mary Poppins* on digital videodisc. Sales were brisk, and at least one film critic listed it among the first ten DVD purchases every family should make after they acquired that new contraption, the DVD player.

This left many American families contemplating a situation of considerable irony. They already had *Mary Poppins* books, and they had *Mary Poppins* videos. Some even had old *Mary Poppins* LP's from their childhood, when they had first heard Julie Andrews sing about a spoonful of sugar. Now they could have *Mary Poppins* in a whole new format.

What they didn't have, though, was the thing they hotly desired: Mary Poppins herself—a baby-sitter who was bright, who cheered everyone up, who somehow brought an unharmonious household into tune. "Where Are You, Mary Poppins?" wailed a columnist in *The Boston Globe* in familiar parental distress. A *Los Angeles Times* author and mother detailed her years spent "in search of Mary Poppins."

Mary Poppins does exist in America. There are talented

people one could hire in this country to love and nurture one's children. They may not resemble the London Mary Poppins—they may come from Ohio, or Barbados—but they are people who can do all the things Americans need for their families. But sadly, they are not people we are often able to hire. And the baby-sitters we can hire are often something less than the film ideal. They are day-care centers where staffs shift too frequently for our two-year-olds. Or they are stay-at-homes with so many problems we end up mothering them as much as our children. Although it embarrasses them to do it, families with baby-sitters frequently find themselves stopping to ask themselves: "Who is my baby-sitter, really?"

The problem of the imperfect baby-sitter is very often not the baby-sitters' fault. Baby-sitters and day-care staffers today are harassed and underpaid, and often, rightly, resent the deal their employers give them. And they are also something unsavory, something neither they, nor we, like to admit. They are a tax dodge, a refuge we escape to in our flight from tax travails.

The Baby-Tax Trap

No loving parents allow themselves to acknowledge that a cold-blooded thing like tax determines the caregiver they pick for their dear ones. We often list other factors—immigration law, high baby-sitter salaries—before we even consider taxes.

But taxes do constrain us. When it comes to child care, ours is a two-faced time, the time of what might be called the baby-tax trap. We may not acknowledge the baby-tax trap, but it is powerful enough to drive many educated and self-possessed parents to make do with something far less than the lady with the umbrella.

Today, as a nation, we are wealthy. Families earn more than we ever did before. We interpret that wealth to mean freedom, and when it comes to four-wheel-drive vehicles, StairMasters, and DVD technology for viewing *Mary Poppins*, it does. We like to pretend to ourselves that that freedom in our choices extends to child care. We survey the array of things available to us and our children—after-school programs, gymnastics camp—and we tell ourselves that what we offer our children was more than what our parents or grandparents could offer us. We pretend we have the means to stay home and be soccer moms, or work part-time, or take a year off, or spend the way we see fit on child care.

This is a pretension that is somehow important to Americans, and one government, and employers, do their best to encourage. They frenetically create programs and laws that *sound* like freedom. Fortune 500 companies offer "flex-time" programs that allow parents to leave work early or arrive late in order to drop off or pick up kids at school. President Bush and a Democratic Congress wrote the Family Leave Act, which for the first time allows fathers to take time off (without pay) at the birth of the child. The Republican party successfully campaigned to take control of Congress in 1994 on a platform whose central showpiece was a child tax credit that was to build that freedom. President and Mrs. Clinton launched their own showpiece, a child-care initiative, with a summit in 1997.

Yet most Americans sense this is a fiction. Many of us *feel* wealthy, as wealthy, nearly, as the stolid Banks family in *Mary Poppins.* Yet we are, still, somehow not the Bankses. We have trouble affording staff. We very often have trouble affording a baby-sitter who doesn't feel like a compromise. The costs mount so high that they even intrude on the most private decision of all—the decision of whether to have an another child.

Other People's Laws

The reason for this is an unexpected one, given that this is a nation that tells itself it lives in a profamily, prowoman age, an age in which a full one half of all children under age five have a mother who works. It is that child-care benefits are mere window dressing on a bigger architecture of laws, an architecture so formidable that it really does shape child rearing. These laws, many tax laws, aren't about child care. They are about a lot of other things: ensuring social justice, collecting revenue for government projects, ensuring American jobs are not stolen by immigrants, and a host of other unknown and unknowable goals. Yet these laws have a very profound effect on child care. They limit choices. They limit child care's availability and make its cost high. They are arbitrary: day-camp tax deductions, for example, are allowed as "child care," but the tax code's authors have deemed overnight camp a luxury for the well-to-do and it gets no break.

To know the extent to which taxes affect child rearing, take, for starters, the families in which one parent, mom or dad, actually wants to stay home. Many families, one suspects, would like this. But tax burdens on the family make staying home a very expensive proposition these days. People used to keep more of their money. In 1948, three quarters of the income of the median family in this country was exempt from tax. By 1983, the same family saw that only one third of its income was free from tax. The big tax breaks families used to enjoy—the standard deduction and the personal exemption—have not kept pace with the rest of household income. Social Security bills also eat away at family income. All these obligations mean families come up short. Even women who don't want to spend hours or days away from their children often do, to bring home the rent.

Furthermore, tax rules and regulations prescribe the sort of child care Americans should have. They turn us from comfortable people, who pick and chose from a range of affordable options, into frantic people, who must juggle a variety of imperfect solutions, solutions often so deficient as to fuel our guilt.

The High-Priced Nanny

Consider the ideal, the Mary Poppins. She is accessible to the wealthiest among us. And from time to time Americans do hire starchy nannies, whom they pay $250, $500, even $800 a week.

But the costs they pay for this luxury are very high—higher, certainly, than what even the Banks family paid. First recall that the money they pay these dream figures is generally money that is paid *after tax.* We must add to that the costs of Social Security, Medicare, and the unemployment-insurance payments households must make for employees, and the cost grows by thousands. Then there is health insurance—something the responsible employer often wants to offer. None of these items, not even the Social Security, is tax-deductible for the household employer. The result is that maintaining the home is much more expensive than maintaining the office, hardly a situation appropriate to these profamily days. This is so even when one includes the dependent-care credits some families may claim.

To gauge the size of the challenge, it helps to have to take into your hands the actual tax documents that hiring Mary Poppins, or even her equivalent from Mexico City, require of us. The form household employers must file is Schedule H, a four-page document that includes multiple formulas, many more complicated than the formulas on the plain vanilla 1040. There are items that are merely confusing: "Multiply line 21 by 5.4 percent." And there are lines that are actually dizzying: "(f) Multiply col. (c) by .054; (g) Multiply col. (c) by col. (e)." Parents who travel with their baby-sitters have to deal with questions that make them want to run and hide, such as: "Did you pay unemployment contributions to only one state?"

Even more daunting are the dozen-odd pages of instructions that come with the form. Here overtired moms and dads must get into niceties like "sick pay paid to an employee by a third party." There is the question of "deferred compensation." Any home owner who wants to actually set up a pension for his employee faces a morass of challenges. Then there are the jobs the employer must do for the government: the package includes information for parents to distribute to the employee on the Earned Income Credit.

Like most IRS documents, the cover of the pamphlet that comes with Schedule H *looks* friendly. But it is designed specifically to frighten people into compliance. The picture shows a little house with a dog, a rake, and a clothesline waving in the wind. The implication is clear: if you employ anyone to walk Rover, to wash clothes, or to run your leaf blower, you may have to file a Schedule H—or else.

In fact, the Schedule H cover is something of a scaremonger. The IRS has ruled that if you use an outside service with its own supplies to do some of these things, you don't have to file Schedule H. But it has also said that lots of people we hire aren't outside services: nannies, usually, or caregivers for seniors.

Schedule H is an example of the tax code imposing another of its double standards. The law mandates that home employers *act* paternal. It penalizes those who don't file Schedule H. It chastises, fines, and even—although rarely—prosecutes families that don't follow the Social Security laws to the letter. It sends them frightening notices to post over the kitchen phone that inform their employees of their "rights." In short, it asks of the family that it be a business, a well-run business. Very few families are up to that.

Yet, as families know, the laws give these same family employers none of the breaks an actual business would get for doing the very same things. That's because tax law says that household employees are a luxury. At work, a secretary who calls and reserves a table for her boss's tax-deductible lunch is a legal tax deduction. At home, the same person doing baby-sitting is not—even if her employer works scripting Java in the home while she sweeps around the high chair.

Some families do choose to live with the double standard. There are fathers and mothers all over the country who go on-line hunting for nanny tax tips, who consult with their accountants, who buy "nanny handbooks" and take on the challenge. Most working couples don't have that time or money. And the choices that remain have many shortcomings.

Criminal Parents

The first and most common choice is to simply bypass the whole affair and go underground. Off-the-books arrangements also dispense with another nanny problem— proving the foreign nanny has immigration papers. This is a solution that is bad for many employees, who lose the Social Security option available to most other Americans. And it exacts a toll from the families who employ them.

That is because almost every parent who employs babysitters or gardeners off the books feels a little guilty. Most Americans are proud to consider themselves law-abiding people. They teach their children to abide by the law too. Yet here they are, breaking the law in that moral epicenter of their lives, their home.

Nobody relishes the idea of being unmasked as a scofflaw by his child. And since there are very few households in which children do not, eventually, discover most every secret, most children do eventually uncover the fact that their parents have cheated. They may figure it out very late— when they are considering how to pay for child care of their own, for example. But they figure it out.

Going underground, as many working families do, also has its direct costs. Anyone who wants to claim the dependent-care credit for the family caregiver, a small break in the context of all the bills children generate, must supply that person's Social Security number to get the family money back. The Internal Revenue Service is so eager for its money that it has even set up a special arrangement for workers without Social Security numbers—illegal aliens, mostly. These workers establish a special proxy–Social Security number, with which employer and employee file.

One may well wonder about this. Does applying for one of these proxy numbers set off bells at the immigration service and get the nanny deported? Not usually. The IRS wants its money so much that it has actually made it policy not to tell the Immigration and Naturalization Service what it's doing. This odd cooperation may suit the two government agencies, but it certainly puts families in an unnerving gray area. They have to remember to keep up the lie with the INS, while scrupulously reporting the truth to the tax hounds.

Finally, for many professionals, having a black-market nanny means risking a career. Both Zoe Baird and Kimba Wood, President Clinton's nominees for attorney general, lost their chance at being the nation's first female attorney general when it emerged that they had "nanny problems." Baird paid immigrants off the books—a tax and immigration problem. Judge Wood hired a foreigner before that became clearly illegal. Still, this was enough, in these days of political hypersensitivity, to taint her candidacy.

A Nation of Scofflaws

The whole arrangement is also a punishing one for employees. They face their own obstacles to on-the-books work. In periods of higher unemployment, our nation's social planners have often wondered why baby-sitter demand can't be matched up with jobless labor. Down on the ground, this argument looks ridiculous. Unemployed people and borderline earners often *can't afford* to make more money. As the social critic Charles Murray observed long ago in his landmark book, *Losing Ground,* their benefits are contingent on their unemployment status. Welfare checks, food stamps, school scholarships, and housing subsidies: all these require low income and start to disappear when a worker makes $15,000 instead of $5,000.

Lawmakers over the years have worked hard to reduce some of these disincentives. But in their place they have created another, even more powerful disincentive, one we have encountered elsewhere: the Earned Income Credit. A baby-sitter who has children of her own and makes $11,000 stands to lose thousands in cash EIC rebates if she takes a job that brings her income up to $25,000. Why, then, should she go to work to take care of someone else's children when she does just as well staying home taking care of her own?

Indeed, entry-level workers who want to be on-the-books baby-sitters are a very scarce commodity indeed. This is because this group generally pays the stiffest penalties for choosing to work. The EIC phases out at $25,000 or $30,000, often the income levels their households begin to hit when they take a nanny job to supplement their husband's. For baby-sitters, therefore, the best solution often seems to be to keep the whole baby-sitting arrangement in the dark. This complicity may satisfy everyone in the short run—after all, few families use nannies for more than five or ten years. But it is a rotten deal for the baby-sitters. It keeps them out of the Social Security program. Though they have worked for years, they often end up retiring with little or no public pension at all.

The consequence of all this is that today there are even more Zoe Bairds and Kimba Woods than there were in the scandalous Nannygate days of the early 1990s. Recently the IRS reported embarrassedly that only one in thirteen tax-payers who owe "nanny taxes" for their baby-sitters or their senior companions actually pay them. This is up from one in eight, the rate a few years ago. This must chagrin law-makers, who actually passed a "baby-sitter" bill after the Zoe-Kimba debacle. But that bill still made expensive taxes due for anyone who spent more than around $1,100 in a year on child care in the home. Most working families will use up $1,100 of child care fast. There are tens of millions of small children in families in America. But only 314,000 households actually chose to follow the law and pay nanny taxes in 1996. Nanny taxes have made us a nation of scofflaws.

The Day-Care Dilemma

Then there is day care, the choice of some three million families. In a day-care arrangement, the center is the employer, so there's none of the tax headache for families. More families want to use day care than can use it. That's because a "good" day-care center, the kind that meets all the government criteria, that guarantees one caregiver for every four children, that follows all the myriad health regulations and tax laws that apply to it, is often very hard to find.

One reason is that our tax laws make it hard for day care

to be profitable. Day care is a labor-intensive business, and as such is indeed heavily taxed. The sheer number of people a day-care center has to employ tends to overwhelm any business-tax advantage. For starters, there are the regular taxes these businesses must carry: Social Security, Medicare, sometimes health benefits. The result is that not many people want to offer day care in the first place. New York City's tax and health laws, for example, have caused a dire shortage of available day care.

Then there are the other hidden day-care taxes. One is lawsuits. Our nation's lawyers and courts have turned child care into a legal minefield. Every time someone sues a day-care center, and people do it all the time, the center pays for that out of its profits or in higher insurance premiums. In the Washington area and its suburbs, day-care centers faced six- and seven-figure lawsuits from families over an allergic reaction to milk (a child who was allergic to milk products drank from another child's cup and died), sexual harassment (a child forced another child to touch his genitals), and over their refusal to administer special injections to children who were allergic to peanuts (the providers weren't trained to do that). Big federal and state agencies reinforce that problem by hounding the agencies with rigid rules on matters ranging from crib size to baby-bottle sanitation.

The day-care shortage is a problem that has proven particularly bitter since we put through welfare reform. Our welfare law now tells young single mothers that they have to work. So they have to find day care. But at the same time government makes that day care hard to find by unloading a mountain of rules and regulations on what day care is acceptable. Besides, many working Americans have second thoughts at the idea of sending their infants off to be rocked at a series of anonymous bosoms. And finally, there is the question of the day-care center fees. A family may well be able to afford one child in day care. But two children in day care usually means double, or near-double, the cost.

The Au Pair Loophole

It's been said that "an economy breathes through it loopholes." Like all other distressing tax situations, the childcare trap has generated a loophole, a picturesque one at that: the au pair.

Au pair means "on the same level as" or "equal to" in French and generally refers to young foreign women who come into a household to help with the child care. Twenty years ago the concept was not commonly known in this country, although we did of course have baby-sitters, live-in college students, and what used to be known as the "summer girl"—an unofficial au pair. The rise of the official, government-sanctioned au pair is a phenomenon of the 1980s and 1990s. In 1986, when the United States Information Agency got started issuing visas for au pairs, mostly from Europe, the total number of official au pairs was something like three hundred. Today that number is twelve thousand and still growing. Young people, mostly female and European, come to live with American families in exchange for baby-sitting services. They are visible—nineteen-, twenty-, twenty-one-year-old girls who look too young to be mothers strapping recalcitrant toddlers into car seats in parking lots all over suburbia.

Au pairs have several obvious attractions. One is that they are foreign, a fact that charms parents interested in importing a bit of culture into their homes. What's cuter than a toddler who can lisp *"Bonne nuit"*? Another is that they aren't servants, a fact that appeals to Americans' egalitarian nature.

But au pairs have other advantages that are worth a lot in the pricey world of child care. The biggest is that the government is willing to engage in a little creative deception and pretend these workers aren't workers. Our laws say that au pairs are cultural guests, exchange students who come to bathe in American culture. The United States Information Agency, the part of the federal government that administers the program, treats the arrangement like a cultural exchange and even calls it such; the message it gives to European teens who apply is that they will stay with a family and get to know the country. Au pairs even get a small stipend toward "education," $500 or so, enough to take a course here or there.

Because au pairs are not, officially, workers, au pair families don't have to deal with Schedule H, the household-employee problem, or the challenge of paying into someone's Social Security account for years. They don't have to worry about unemployment taxes or those alarming notices state governments send out reading "Post for All Employees." They don't have to worry about the expense of health insurance, because the au pair agency takes care of that. All they must do is pay a flat fee to the agency and give their au pair a stipend of, to use the going rate, $139 a week. Finally, they do not have to worry about their au pair's future, the way they would with a real employee. After a year their au pair, and her future, will be safely back in Denmark or France. And it's all legal.

To frustrated families, the foreign au pair loophole brings

powerful relief. It lifts all the burdens—tax and regulatory, but principally tax—that employing a plain old American involves. Foreigners also use au pairdom as a loophole around immigration law. A one-year visa to hang out in the United States is hard to get. The au pair arrangement makes it suddenly easy. Europe has terrible unemployment, and many teenagers there have no prospect anywhere as glamorous as the idea of spending a year learning English in middle-class America. And, indeed, most au pair relationships don't turn out badly. Many turn out well.

Louise Woodward's Case

But the au pair arrangement, even the successful one, really isn't true cultural exchange. It may be *called* cultural exchange, but it is actually a gentrified form of colonial indenture. Families who get au pairs—hire them, really—often expect the new arrival to be more like an employee. They are told to expect up to forty hours of full-time rigorous baby-sitting, the sort of schedule that would be a challenge to anyone who is not Mary Poppins.

Recently a murder case in Massachusetts provided dramatic and tragic demonstration of the limits of the au pair. A baby named Matthew Eappen was left in the care of Louise Woodward, a young au pair from Elton, England. While in her care, the baby went into convulsions, and then a coma from which he never emerged. At this point no one knows what caused Matthew Eappen's death: a jury convicted Louise Woodward, but the judge sent her home to England.

What the case did make clear was that this baby-sitter

from England fell short of the gentle English ideal. She took too many nights out attending the musical *Rent,* she failed to wake to care for the Eappen children, and she spent plenty of time on the phone, leaving the children unattended. Even before the tragic incident, the Eappens were unhappy with their au pair and had handed her several ultimatums.

The story was typical of the clash of expectations over au pairs. After the trial, Penelope Leach, one of our society's reigning child-care gurus, condemned the whole affair in an op-ed article in *The New York Times* titled "Children Minding Children." "Child care," wrote Ms. Leach, "isn't what au pairs have come for or what they really want to do. Au pairs are available to American parents because young women from other countries want to spend time in the United States, not because they want to be with children or even because they want a job."

Millions of families who do not have official au pairs find themselves in the Eappens' shoes. Nothing is good enough, so they must make do. One reason women are ambivalent about day care is, of course, that they are ambivalent about leaving their children in the first place. But another is that they are right in suspecting their child is not getting enough attention. Their fears are legitimate. Given what we are able to pay for day care, we do need videocams and telephone beepers to monitor our caregivers.

As with all tax distortions, baby taxes do benefit someone, or several someones. The first is independent service firms. If you hire one of these—a "lawn doctor" or a "maid service"—you are contracting independently and need not deal with the mountain of tax paperwork. (But beware: the

IRS has dozens of criteria for determining if someone actually is an employee, and it loves to test them. If your house has a broom and a mop and your cleaning lady uses them instead of bringing her own, you flunk.) Day-care centers also fall into this class. Parents are so eager to shift the burden of the nanny laws onto someone that they pay a premium to those centers that are available. The equity markets even show evidence of this: KinderCare, a national baby-sitting chain, is a publicly traded stock.

It wasn't always this way. For most of the nation's history, tax law made it easier to be a household employer. People didn't have to pay taxes, so they had more of it to spend. One of the things they did was employ servants. Census Bureau data show that in 1910 a full 7 percent of the nonfarm workforce was employed in private households. Most of these people were housekeepers, but "privately employed laundresses" were close to 1 percent of the workforce at that point.

Long before the income tax came to touch the modern family, the nanny trap was laid when economists and politicians wrote our nation's tax law. Business was business, the law said: expenses in business should be fully deductible. The home, though, was different: expenses there were luxuries, to be paid in after-tax dollars. Of course, it is important to recall that pre-tax dollars were not such a precious thing in the old days. That's because the income tax didn't touch most families. All of their dollars were pre-tax dollars.

Then along came the income tax, which made pre-tax money precious and scarce. Right away, families began trying to recapture some of that money. In 1939, just a few years before the income tax affected average Americans, a career couple named Smith tried to claim deductions for the child care that they paid while at work. The nation's courts had a response to this. The Smiths didn't have to have children. Their decision, and their need, was "inherently personal." There was a second message, perhaps unintended, that the Smith case sent: a wife's work is a luxury.

Very soon after this, lawmakers began making allowances for child care. Over the years various credits and deductions became allowable. But often they were only available to lower and middle earners. The maximum child credit available to middle-class and upper-middle-class families today is worth less than $5,000.

In the 1990s the Republican party made a huge show of righting all this. One of the items in the Contract with America, the Republican agenda for 1994, was the child-care credit. In 1997 the child-care credit did pass, as part of the questionably named Taxpayer Relief Act.

But many families were very disappointed with the credit. The first reason was that there was a delay in its effect: it only began in 1998, a full four years after Republicans were voted into the majority in the House of Representatives on the strength of their child-care promises.

More disappointing than the delay was that it was of little value to families. For one thing, the credit, at $500 when phased in, was too small to matter much to the average two-earner family. Its median income was $53,650 in 1996, meaning that the Republicans' much cherished credit made a difference of less than 1 percent in the finances of the average working family. Even one-earner families, which earn a median of $35,304, would hardly note the difference.

Then there is the credit's puny size when compared with

the cost of full-time child care. The very cheapest of child care costs $100 a week or more; Louise Woodward made $115, plus her room and board. That means the credit was equal to about one tenth of the money any family that seriously uses child care might require. Even more hurtful, the child-care credit phases out. When families became too successful, they no longer received the money. The tax message to working mothers was, effectively: if you work a little, we will give you a break. If you work a lot or succeed at your work, you will have to pay for it. Our tax structure means that while we may earn like the nineteenth-century bourgeoisie, we may not live like them.

Many Americans tolerate all this out of a perverse sort of sense of *noblesse oblige*—or, at the very least, *bourgeoisie oblige*. Anyone who desires household help, they say to themselves, desires servants. And having servants isn't an egalitarian, modern, thing to do. Yet if parents feel they want someone talented, someone warm, someone capable in their homes, why shouldn't they be able to hire that person? What makes a factory job a "good job" for a lower earner to have, and a baby-sitting job a "bad job"? Lower taxes, moreover, would enable families, as employers, to pay their baby-sitters more. Why should our children lose out because of outdated, misplaced, Great Society guilt?

There's yet another force, not directly a tax force but a related one, that puts families against the wall. It is immigration law. In the early 1990s the nation was in a recession, and downsizing frightened American families. It also gave fuel to the anti-immigrant forces in Congress, who responded to the whole matter by slapping new controls on unskilled workers from abroad—precisely the group many

Americans hire as nannies. Unemployment, in the mean-
time, has dropped to historic lows. The nation needs labor.
But the law stands. And an army of INS officials keeps
busy, slowing down the process enabling the baby-sitters to
work legally.

The most compelling evidence that working families—
all families, indeed—are unhappy with child care is an absence: a missing child. Many of today's young parents come
from three- and four-child families and would like to have
two or three children themselves. Yet they stick with one or
two because having that extra child is simply "too much." It
is "too much" in part because of careers, concerns about
overpopulation, what the papers call "lifestyle choices," but
also because of cost—cost often generated by taxes. Many
families mark the day on their mental calendar when they
can stop hiring baby-sitters. Having another child moves
that day further forward. Families who have their children
in private schools pay double tuition for each child—once
through the taxes they pay for that child's place in public
school, even though he does not occupy it. How many people have we heard saying, "We just couldn't afford another
child"?

As long as high taxes cut at families' freedom, the struggle will continue. The nation's au pair loophole will keep
expanding. Anxious parents will indeed buy concealable
videocams on the off chance of espying baby-sitter abuses,
and they will race home early to see that everyone is all
right. And they will continue to keep asking themselves, as
the Eappens must have, where is Mary Poppins? And, who
is my baby-sitter, really?

7

YOUR SCHOOL

IN FEBRUARY OF 1997 A THIRTY-EIGHT-YEAR-OLD MOTHER of three from East Dorset, Vermont, called her state representative with a question. She had heard on the news that Vermont's supreme court had declared the local school-funding system unconstitutional. The woman, whose name was Mary Barrosse, had two daughters in Dorset Elementary School, Rosie and Gracie. She had another child entering nursery school. Part of the reason she and her husband, a doctor with a family practice, had made their home in East Dorset was because the district invested heavily in its schools. What exactly did the change mean?

Mary Barrosse's representative, a man named Walt Freed, did not give her good news. Vermont's courts had overturned the state's longstanding system of school finance. Under the old system, town property taxes paid directly for something like three quarters of the cost of local schools. Now, at least for a while, the towns would still collect the money. But they would have to send it along to the state, which would set property-tax rates for everyone and then return a flat block grant of $5,000 or so per child to each town for education.

The court had said it would no longer be all right for one school district to spend more money on its children than another. That wasn't giving Vermont children an equal opportunity to learn. The court acknowledged that the system of local property taxes paying for local schools was old but said that it must be ended. It said today's children "cannot be limited by eighteenth-century standards." It referred to *Brown* v. *Board of Education,* the landmark federal case that had taken on school segregation. Vermont didn't have a race problem—99 percent of its population was white. But the court likened the school-spending disparities to racial discrimination. Its message was serious: social justice on a grand scale was involved here. The money had to go to the state capital so that it could be given out fairly. Equal spending was to be.

The Meddling Hand

Schools and how we pay for them are things Americans feel strongly about. Over the course of the past three decades, state courts and governments like Vermont's have moved repeatedly in the name of equity to change how schools are financed. For equity's sake, they have fiddled with the local connection parents have with their schools. And every time they have done so, they have met with curiosity, incomprehension, and even fury from parents. In this case it is not the greed of the greedy hand that so troubles us. It is its meddling.

Even if, like Mary Barrosse, we have never been particularly interested in taxes before, school problems set us thinking about them, even turning us political. Her story is worth following for what it tells us about ourselves and the way we react when government—local, state, or federal—changes an intimate thing like the way we educate our children. We begin to wonder: why is this happening? And where is the money going? And, why didn't someone ask me?

Over the months that followed her first telephone call to Walt Freed, Vermont's legislature moved to implement the court's ruling, and Mary Barrosse tried to figure out where she stood. She learned that there were many in Vermont's state legislature who agreed with the ruling and had pushed for the supreme court case. Many of the lawmakers were teachers, members of teachers' families, or school administrators, who thought Montpelier would do a better job of controlling the money. Others had even campaigned on the theme, arguing that the new regime would cut property taxes. Many Democrats generally backed the change, and many Republicans opposed it, but it wasn't entirely a partisan debate: some Republicans supported the switch; some Democrats opposed it. The governor, Howard Dean, was proud of the change and would later call the new era of statewide funding "a joyous time."

It became clear to Barrosse that, now that the supreme court had ruled, party line and individual decisions didn't matter much. Even those lawmakers who opposed the change had little choice now but to join in undertaking a sort of Robin Hood action to help poorer Vermont towns. It soon became clear too that the state probably needed to raise property taxes for many Vermonters, particularly those who lived in wealthier towns, if it was to implement the court's order. Representative Freed reported to Barrosse that it looked like some of the wealthier towns' school money would probably now go to subsidize towns with lower tax bases. The budgets of the schools in the wealthier towns would probably have to be cut.

Barrosse's Cuts

At home, Barrosse found herself contemplating what might be cut at Dorset Elementary. Her area spent several thousands over the $5,100 cap the state was imposing. Yet her school didn't have a cafeteria, so spending couldn't be reined in there. It did have a health teacher, and it had a relatively low student-teacher ratio. She put down the phone and worried. She had never thought at length about school finance or property taxes, and she wished the problem would go away. She remembers thinking, "They can keep their taxes. Just let us have our schools."

Indeed, the state legislature's plan, known as Act 60, sounded less like a Robin Hood scenario than simply robbing Peter to pay Paul. Under the new statewide property-tax rules, citizens would pay $1,100 for every $100,000 in assessed value on their property. For low-income owners, this rate would be lowered. But for those with considerable property—the five-hundred-acre farmer—there was no escape from a giant tax hike from the state. If towns wanted to spend more than their block grant, they could raise that extra money on their own. But they had to give a share of every additional dollar they raised to poorer towns.

It also became clear that Act 60 would split Vermont's 251 towns into two groups: "receiving towns," which would benefit from the subsidy, and "sending towns," which were deemed prosperous enough to part with their money. In

Montpelier lawmakers spoke with a touch of schadenfreude about the wealthy towns sharing their prosperity; "gold towns," thriving ski resorts for the most part, were to be among some of the biggest "senders."

Dorset was clearly going to be a "sender," a sender that had to undertake serious cuts. Yet later in 1997, when lawmakers passed Act 60, the law enforcing the supreme court decision, the scope of the cuts shocked Barrosse. The health teacher would indeed be laid off. So would two classroom teachers, raising the student-teacher ratio at Dorset Elementary to about twenty to one from fifteen to one. Technical education and shop classes would end. Other cuts were coming in music, art, computers. Then there was gym. Altogether, Dorset Elementary School's budget was to be cut 30 percent. But actually, the cuts would feel deeper. State and federal law said the school could not cut its special-education programs for handicapped children. The superintendent's budget—administrative jobs—also were not to be touched. So all that 30 percent had to come out of the regular classroom. Teacher salaries would have to come down. This after local parents had worked very hard to recruit the teachers with competitive salaries.

Barrosse, whose third child, Bernie, was due to enter kindergarten after all these cuts were in place, pondered the situation over and over. She thought about private school, but it was costly, and there wasn't really a good school near her that seemed right for her kids. She had another question for Walt Freed. She had heard the news that towns could spend above the flat rate at town schools if they levied extra property taxes for that purpose. In 1998 her property taxes would be something like $3,100. How much, she asked

Freed, would her property taxes need to go up if Dorset wanted to maintain its current budget? Freed told her Dorset would have to double her property tax to something like $6,200 just to sustain the school the way it was. Towns like Stratton and Winhall would face an even greater challenge. They would have to raise taxes up to seven times in order to keep the schools they currently had.

"This Clean, Safe Place"

Barrosse couldn't believe what she was hearing. When they were younger, she and her husband had bounced about the world. Before Vermont, they had lived in Japan, where her husband had paid off the bills for his medical school by serving as a doctor with the military. They had seen Vermont as their haven, their refuge, the place they chose to make their nest. "This was this clean, safe place, a place where you can be friends with everybody," Barrosse recalls.

Now she began to read about the school-tax problem in earnest. She learned that the legislation was sometimes called "equalization," and that it had happened all over New England. Maine had had its equalization story in the 1970s; New Hampshire was expecting its supreme court to call for change sometime later in 1997. Equalization had happened on the West Coast too, and in Texas. All over the country, citizens were fighting treacherous, violent little battles over the changes. Barrosse was a writer and a painter, and now she was fairly busy being a mother. Originally she had come from Wilmington, Delaware. Like many of Vermont's transplants—including members of the legislature who had pushed for equalization—she knew she wanted opportunity for all kids. Surely, equal opportunity for kids was not wrong.

A NIMBY Reaction

Yet the equalization decision still didn't make sense to Mary Barrosse. When she and her husband had first shopped for houses, they had looked at a farm in Danby, not far from Dorset. It was fifty acres, and it was their dream farm. "We could get some sheep," she recalled thinking, "and have this total rural experiment. We were totally primed for that kind of existence." Danby didn't have good schools, though, and good schools were important to them. So they had bought a two-acre place in East Dorset, where they could take advantage of the Dorset area's excellent schools. Now someone from outside—Montpelier—was changing the terms of their situation, without warning them and without asking their permission. The more she thought about it, the angrier she got. Barrosse, who had never thought of herself as a not-in-my-backyard sort of person, now began to feel a sort of NIMBY reaction setting in. The issue wouldn't stay out of her mind. "This was just so wrong."

Barrosse started phoning around, and she found that many of her friends felt the way she did. There were things they didn't like about the state's schools. They weren't happy, for example, that the state had no strong regime for testing kids, which meant there was no barometer to tell how Vermont was doing in education. But there was also a lot to like about Vermont's public schools. The state and towns already spent an average of more than $6,800 per child on education, a thousand dollars above the national average. Were Vermont's schools really so bad that the whole system needed to be ripped up?

Many of the unhappy parents were people in "gold towns," towns for which the state was planning little property-tax bombs. One of them was John Irving, the author of *The World According to Garp.* Irving's five-year-old was just starting school, and he was furious at the change. "Like a lot of families in this area, this choice came for us because of the schools. Now we are seeing those schools decimated," he told a reporter. As a Democrat, he was angry at the Democrats who supported the change. "I'm to the left of most of these people. This is my party that's wreaking havoc." He saw the whole thing as ill-conceived class warfare against the gold towns, class warfare that wasn't even going to work. He said he was thinking of pulling his son out of the public schools.

"Pathological Redistributionists"

But Barrosse also found people in the receiving towns who were angry. Jeffrey Wennberg, the mayor of Rutland, a receiving town, was furious. "These are a bunch of pathological redistributionists," he said. Vermont to him was like a house, a dear house that he had moved to and loved and made his home. But the legislature didn't see that, and implemented the court ruling with shocking vehemence. "They wanted to change things, but they didn't change them incrementally. They just blew up the whole house." Because Rutland was not a gold town, some taxpayers would get small relief. Wennberg had run the numbers and saw that families with incomes between $50,000 and $75,000 might pay $200 or $300 less than they had before. Lower-income families, perversely, would not gain anything. They would save under Act 60's property tax but would lose all that money because the program weakened an older tax abatement for working families. He found that only something like one thousand households of the six thousand paying taxes would get a net tax cut. What was the value of one in six? Why? Worse yet would be the effect on the general economy. Many Rutlanders worked at Killington, the ski resort ten miles down the road. And Killington's taxes were set to double under the arrangement.

All of these people felt that equalization's advocates in Montpelier and in the courts had a hidden agenda: that they were using the equity argument to get control of the property-tax kitty. This argument was hard to ignore. Property taxes represented an additional $680 million, a figure that was higher than Montpelier's revenues from all the other state taxes combined. Legislators were already bragging about their new clout. "Money follows power," commented Wennberg bitterly.

At summer's end, while picking apples for her son's nursery school, Barrosse talked with other mothers. They had heard that Governor Dean was hosting a meeting of Democratic governors at the Equinox, a historic inn in Manchester. It was well known that Governor Dean supported Act 60. Barrosse and the other mothers decided they would do something.

Outside the Equinox, standing on the back of a red pickup truck that belonged to Barrosse's husband, protestors talked about why they were unhappy with the change.

Even though the night was cold—"we held candles and shivered," Barrosse recalls—more than five hundred people showed up, many more than anyone had anticipated. The number sounded small, but it was one of the biggest political rallies in Vermont in years. The state had called out volunteer firefighters, with hoses, in case the event was too rough. The protestors carried signs that made puns, like SOURED ON HOWARD. One speaker played on the fact that the governor was a medical doctor. She asked him "if one leg was broken, would you break the other to equalize the pain?" They talked about how the "equalized yield pool," the technical language for the change, was really a "shark pool."

The Equinox event resonated in Vermont, in part precisely because it took place at the Equinox. Vermonters knew that the hotel stood on the site of an old tavern that had been there since colonial days, when the Green Mountain Boys met to plot their battle against the British in the American Revolution. The governor's inadvertent choice of the location was a bitter reminder of what Montpelier's work was doing to Vermont's old tradition of home rule. In revolutionary times Vermont was so independent that it did the rest of America one better. After the thirteen colonies revolted against Britain, Vermont revolted against the thirteen colonies and became the fourteenth state.

For more than two hundred years, Vermont's tiny towns had conducted their business on an annual town-meeting day. In many towns every citizen is allowed to vote on the budget. "This is a state where ninth-graders know Robert's Rules of Order," says Walt Freed. All Vermont watched as the lawmakers wrote Act 60, the implementing law. In late

June 1997, or soon after Act 60, the state's education department asked a polling company called Macro to survey voters on their opinions. Of those surveyed, 42 percent said that they thought Act 60 was "unlikely" to bring "substantially equal educational opportunity" to Vermont, while 46 percent said it was "likely." By October the tide was turning: 50 percent said the change was "unlikely" to achieve its goals, compared with 40 percent who still thought it could work. One in four thought that the program was "unlikely" to benefit even the children in poorer towns.

Soon Vermont's towns, which had never felt particularly divided before, did indeed find themselves pitted against one another into two opposing armies, an army of haves and an army of have-nots. *The New York Times,* which sent a reporter to cover Act 60 and its reception, quoted Louis Costanza, a retiree from Long Island, who expected the property tax on his three-bedroom home in Winhall to go to $6,000 from $800. "They see a lot of Mercedes and Land Rovers and Wagoneers and say: 'Those yuppies have a lot of money. How am I going to get it?' They've been dreaming about this for a long time." The story also related a NIMBY anecdote. Cameron Page, a Stowe mother and school-board member, met a woman from a receiving town at a hockey match. Page told the *Times* that the neighbor "actually leaned over to me and said, 'Nyeh, nyeh.'"

There were those, though, who expressed their anger in a more direct fashion. Vermont, the self-advertised "picture postcard" state, began to see outright hostility. Cheryl Rivers, a state senator who had led the writing of Act 60 from the legislature's finance committee, was one of the targets. She sold her old Dodge Colt, only to learn that opponents of property-tax change were the buyers. They parked the car in front of the statehouse and offered bypassers a chance to hit it with a baseball bat. The price was $5 a whack. Vermont, Mary Barrosse's clean, safe place, where everyone could be friends with everyone, was moving toward civil war.

An American Reaction

The Vermonters' property-tax reaction was, in its way, a classically American event. Property taxes have always been important to Americans, often more important than most of the other taxes we pay. This has been true since the days of the colonies. In 1768 citizens from North Carolina's Orange and Rowan counties warned that "a few shillings in taxes might seem trifling to gentlemen roiling in affluence, but to Poor People who must have their Bed and Bedclothes, yea their Wives Petticoats taken and sold to Defray [taxes] how Tremenjouse judge must be the consequences." Fries' rebellion, one of several early tax revolts that shook the young nation, was a property-tax rebellion; thirty traitors were convicted and two sentenced to death, but President Adams pardoned them all.

After this bumptious start, though, things grew more peaceful. One reason this was so is that those property taxes soon came to be spent on something people cherished— their town schools. A hundred years ago property taxes and schools were a very local affair in most states. What we imagine of the arrangement—four farmers meeting on a village green to pay for a schoolmistress, who also lodged at their houses—is not inaccurate. Vermont's first constitution, from 1777, reflected this vision by making local funding the explicit rule: "A school or schools shall be established in each town, by the legislature, for the convenient instruction of youth, with such salaries to the masters to be paid by the town; making proper use of school lands in each town, thereby to enable them to instruct youth at low prices."

Most constitutions were something like this early one: they used phrases like "thorough and efficient" to describe the sort of education they wanted their citizens' children to receive. The implication was that towns would provide that education. A wealthier town might choose to spend more, a poorer town less. That was their business and their lot. In short, a local matter. Alexis de Tocqueville traveled in America in the 1830s, years in which the schools system was beginning to take root. He wrote, "The Americans, on the other hand, are fond of explaining almost all the actions of their lives by the principle of self-interest, rightly understood; they show with complacency how an enlightened regard for themselves constantly prompts them to assist one another and inclines them willingly to sacrifice a portion of their time and property to the welfare of the state." He was referring, mostly, to religion. But the local schools that developed after he wrote were a prime example of what he called "self-interest, rightly understood."

Economists and education scholars have additional explanations for all this contentment. They say it is because a local property tax, spent locally, is a "good tax." People who pay property taxes for schools they control see what they are getting; if they like it, they push to "buy more," and pass or tolerate tax increases. If they don't like it, they will try to "buy" less from government by pushing for a tax cut. "Local property taxes, spent locally, are a fee-for-service arrangement disguised as a tax," says William Fischel, a professor at Dartmouth who studied the effects of equalization.

The Tiebout Hypothesis

In their explanations of school funding, the economists often refer to something called the Tiebout hypothesis, after Charles Tiebout, a scholar of public finance. In the 1950s Tiebout tried to work out what happened in suburban towns. He found and articulated what most Americans already know instinctively: towns compete for families, through their schools, their parks, their safety records. People, in simple language, will "vote with their feet." They will give up more space, as Mary Barrosse did, for better schools. They will choose Dorset over Danby.

This competition has a very healthy effect on almost everyone. It allows the Danbys to choose not to invest in public schools, if they like. But that choice brings its own punishment: so few people are attracted to the Danbys that there aren't enough people around with valuable homes. Those who are there have to pay extra property taxes because there are fewer people to shoulder the burden. The result is the situation in many of Vermont's poorer towns: high property-tax rates.

But the Tiebout rule helps the Dorsets, setting off a virtuous cycle there. People like to move to places like Dorset, and they do that in numbers. When enough of them do so, there are more people around to share the burden of school costs. If a town like Dorset attracts enough home owners, and values of homes go up enough, citizens can then have their cake and eat it too. They get high property values, low tax rates, and good schools.

This is good for everyone in Dorset. It is good for lower-income people and renters, since they get the benefit of good schools. It is even good for empty-nesters who pay lots of property taxes and have no children in school. In the end they collect their benefit from the situation when they sell their house, at a higher price than they might in a town with bad schools. Caroline Hoxby, a Harvard economist who studied school finance, put it this way: "You don't have to care about education. You just have to know that the people who might buy your house care about education." The Scarsdales, Oak Parks, and Palo Altos of this world were evidence of the Tiebout hypothesis. Chester Finn, an education scholar and official in President Bush's education department, spelled the phenomenon out in noneconomic terms: "When they know what they are getting, there is no amount people won't spend for their children's education."

The Supreme Court Speaks

Gradually, though, in this century, federal government and states began to cut at the local connection and undermine Tiebout's virtuous cycle. They started to foot some of the costs of education. In the 1950s and 1960s, the issue of funding came up in the nation's civil rights discussion. Schools in cities' poor neighborhoods often had less to offer their students than the plush schools in the suburbs. In Washington, the U.S. Supreme Court addressed this issue by handing down the opinions that gave the nation busing. And states and the federal government often paid for that busing. Very soon, though, it became clear that busing was not ending inequality in America. So civil rights advocates tried another way. They argued before the Supreme Court that every child across the nation was entitled to equal spending under the equal-protection clause of the Constitution.

Our nation's top justices would not go that far. In a famous case, *Rodriguez,* they refused to say that every locality must spend the same amount on every child, or that school finance must be rearranged to make that possible. Lewis Powell wrote that education "is not among the rights afforded explicit protection under our Federal constitution." So the civil rights forces in the states tried another route. They sued under their state's constitutions. A report on their very first case, brought in the 1970s, can be found on a Web site Act 60 opponents created to talk about their problem with one another, act60.org. Called *Serrano* v. *Priest,* the case challenged California's education system. It said all parts of California must spend about the same amount per child on education. This meant, in the words of one economist who looked at the matter, that "tax-financed differences in spending per pupil were, for all practical purposes, eradicated." After *Serrano,* California ended its old local property-tax system. It planned to force richer neighborhoods to subsidize poorer neighborhoods. This meant that, at least in the short run, schools would be more equal.

But *Serrano* killed the virtuous cycle in California. It meant that families started to lose control of what they were getting for the money. Like Mary Barrosse, Californians felt rooked. When that arrangement broke down, people started to get angry. And they started to check out.

Nowhere was this more visible than in California in the years after *Serrano*. Californians were losing control of their local schools. They didn't want to pay more. The consequence was a property-tax revolt unlike any that had occurred in postwar America: "Mad as hell" was the slogan Howard Jarvis, the revolt's leader, used to sum up Californians' rage. "I forgot all about where I was and what I was doing and fixed, like tunnel vision, on the bill," said one California home owner to a researcher, describing the moment she received news of a 250 percent increase in her property tax. "Inside I got hysterical . . . I was filled with fear and also with anger, and it was such a mix of emotions that I just stood there, and I think I vibrated for about ten minutes." School equalization so angered them that it moved Californians to pass Proposition 13, a draconian law capping and freezing property taxes. Their rage was so powerful that it had national consequences, setting off the only genuine national tax-cutting movement in the country since World War II, a movement that brought about the income tax cuts of the 1980s.

The *Serrano*–Prop 13 connection was not something observers at the time chose to focus on. Some of them blamed another, and very genuine, problem of the period: inflation. Economists like Michael Boskin, who later became chairman of the President's Council of Economic Advisers, pointed out that the 1970s were years of wild property appreciation in California. When the value of Californians' homes went up, their property taxes rose too. The cap in Proposition 13 effectively checked that, for a while.

Others explained Prop 13 as simple class warfare. They dismissed Californians as mere selfish suburbanites, an uncaring group who had no interest in supporting their less fortunate neighbors. Two researchers who published a book on the California uprising, David Sears and Jack Citrin, reached this conclusion. The subtitle of their work, *Tax Revolt,* was *Something for Nothing in California.* They and many others argued that the California revolt was simply an ugly foretaste of the 1980s, Ronald Reagan's era of greed.

Serrano's Copycats

Even as the scholars parsed California, though, *Serrano* began to replicate itself. It begat copycat suits. Texas had its *Serrano* case. So did Maine and New Mexico. Later came New Jersey, Kentucky, and Ohio. Usually, the American Civil Liberties Union helped out in making the case for equalization. And usually they started with a set-piece example of inequality in their state. In Vermont, for example, Robert Gensburg, the lead plaintiff's attorney in Brigham, noted that Hardwick, a relatively poor town, found that it had to lay off a remedial-reading teacher for the first grade. He contrasted Hardwick with Stowe, where the town was voting on whether to appropriate $84,000 to repair the high school's tennis courts. In all these states, and soon they came to number over twenty, the goal was the same: power to the state capital, so that it might regulate and enforce equal spending.

While Vermonters struggled over their predicament, one of the more dramatic chapters of the equalization drama was taking place right next door to them, in New Hampshire, a state whose residents had long been famous for their refusal to allow income and sales taxes. Local property taxes paid for almost all its schooling. And the result was formidable. New Hampshire spent more than most states on education. And its students performed better than almost any in the country. It was a national education model, and voters liked it that way.

They had demonstrated their contentment as recently as 1992. In that year a Democratic candidate for governor, Debora "Arnie" Arneson, campaigned on a platform of introducing an income tax. Part of the purpose of the tax was to pay for education. Arneson's supporters promised that many New Hampshirites would pay less under the new regime. Her opponent, Stephen Merrill, opposed a change.

Arneson lost, badly. This was not an unusual vote. Voters of other states also rejected plans to take away local funding. They did it in Maine in 1977, in Michigan in 1978, and in Colorado in 1972. The *Union Leader,* Manchester's conservative paper, summed up the New Hampshire reaction: "If the people of New Hampshire desired a broad-based tax of any kind, income, sales, or property, they have had ample opportunities to demonstrate such at the ballot box."

Still, in December 1997, New Hampshire had its *Serrano,* a case called *Claremont.* The state supreme court declared the property-tax system unconstitutional. The rage was palpable and bound to grow. "Our New Hampshire way of life is being threatened," wrote Jay Lucas, a Republican candidate for governor. Republicans planned to campaign on it in the year 2000, when the presidential primaries would again put New Hampshire in the spotlight.

Vermonters, too, focused on due process. They were particularly unhappy about the way the change had been imposed. The state supreme court had handed down its ruling even though the state's constitution did not explicitly say that the state was responsible for *paying* for students' education. For that matter, the Vermont constitution didn't even say a word about "equal spending." The case had been based on a clause that said simply that a "competent number of schools ought to be maintained in each town unless the general assembly permits other provisions for the convenient instruction of youth." Even the lead counsel for the plaintiff, Robert Gensburg, noted that when he had first hunted for equality language applicable to schools in the constitution, he found so little that "my heart sank."

As it turned out, though, the Vermont Supreme Court hadn't paid much mind to what the state constitution said. It stretched the language in the state constitution to fit equalization. And it quoted the famous federal case, *Brown v. Board of Education,* as if the U.S. Supreme Court had backed equal spending on all American students through property taxes, which of course it hadn't.

But the Vermont judges didn't care. In their opinion, they even said as much: "While history must inform our constitutional analysis, it cannot bind it." Jeffrey Pascoe, a parent from South Burlington, wrote an outraged article about the state court's decision and posted it on the Act 60 Web site. The article noted that the state court had handed down its decision very fast, so fast that Gensburg later bragged, "This was the fastest briefed, argued, and decided case you will probably ever see in the Vermont Supreme Court."

To make their case, Gensburg and his colleagues had searched Vermont for children in particularly low-spending areas, children whose names could then be given to their case. They had settled on Amanda Brigham, a seven-year-old whose school was a three-room schoolhouse in Whiting, a working-class town not far from Middlebury. Her school didn't spend a lot of money, but it did have some computers, and it did have a student-teacher ratio of fewer than twenty to one. Before the supreme court's decision, it spent $800 less per student than the state average, an amount far less than Dorset would now have to give up per child. People couldn't see why it was right to take away extras like computers in these towns just so that they might be maintained, and a gym might be added, at Amanda Brigham's school. Another receiving area with a low tax base, Essex, had schools whose students scored among the best in the state on standardized tests. Was it really necessary to move money and cut back at other schools to give yet more to this kind of student?

Then there was the evidence that Montpelier was already moving to centralize. Act 60 contained numerous new mandates that the states would impose on schools. It was going to introduce new statewide rules on local standards, set up a new barrage of requirements for the schools, and subject the schools to review every two years by a commissioner to "determine whether students in each Vermont public school are provided educational opportunities substantially equal to those provided in other public schools." The threat to schools that didn't meet the criteria was clear: with its newfound control of the purse, the state could close the school. What particularly irked citizens was that the state was spending quite a lot to pay for its new power center: $5 million to establish the oversight office, for starters.

What upset many Vermonters most, though, was that

there seemed no way of going back. In the winter of 1997 and 1998, some towns were still considering raising property taxes to improve schools. State lawmakers actually discouraged them from doing that—in other words, encouraged them to stay dependent so that they could keep their "receiving" status. Melissa Perkins, a citizen of Shaftsbury, a receiving town, studied the state government's report on her town and discovered it would indeed be saving 11 percent on property taxes. But it also needed to spend an extra $107,388 in compliance costs to get ready for the new system. And it now found itself in an awkward situation. The town had been planning to increase its school spending significantly, by $287,559. But its planners discovered if they did that, they would lose "too much" of Act 60's benefit. Perkins had discovered one of the many perversities in the new law: for towns with lower property-tax bases, it actually discouraged educational spending. Why should they choose to raise property taxes and pay more if it meant risking money and their status as a receiving town? The governor, wrote Perkins, "wants the people of Shaftsbury to spend $107,388 to support Act 60, but not $287,559 to support our children. What's wrong with this picture?"

Tom Watson's Taxes

Rage so moved Fred Schwacke, a member of the Winhall school board, that he penned a long and compelling essay on the Internet, a sort of prose political version of Robert Frost's "The Road Not Taken." "I've driven through Winhall when it was just bad roads in winter," he wrote, recalling troubling times. The state's improvement, he said, was based on important events, like IBM's decision to site jobs in Essex Junction. "Let's not forget that IBM's founder, Tom Watson, loved to ski at Stowe, and that recreational draw is a major reason why Vermont's largest employer was located here," wrote Schwacke, who had two school-age sons. Vermont's ski economy was already being challenged by the rise of skiing in places like western Canada and Idaho. "A point that Montpelier seems to have overlooked, but which is well known in ski country, is the fragile nature of its economy. To see the point just think back to the last bad snow year. Or a little farther to the gas crisis. . . . Look at what effect cutting back or closing a ski area has on the local economy and state revenues. Look at what happened to land values at Magic Mountain when it closed. Put plain and simply, for the most part Vermont's 'gold towns' are perched on a fragile economic base."

Equalization Didn't Work

The saddest part of the story is that even after all its costs, equalization didn't really work. Some extra money did indeed reach poor towns. But those results came at the Tiebout price. Like Californians, the taxpayers in other states going through equalization were angry. They began to push for lower tax rates. In New Mexico and other states, equal spending became the rule, but it was equal spending at a very low level. The change—centralizing, taking away local authority and local people's say—was as much a tax change as a change about equity. Citizens simply resisted the idea of courts telling them how to spend their money, or taking that money far away. They viewed it as a modern form of taxation without representation.

Even in places where spending did go up, the schools still seemed to be in trouble. The federal government, the state of New Jersey, and the city of Newark spend more per child on Newark children than on the children of many of New Jersey's fanciest suburbs. But even with all the spending, the results were not satisfactory. Newark children still failed, and Newark high-schoolers still could not read when they graduated. A soldier in Ohio's equalization war, an adjunct fellow at Ashland University, posted his exasperation on the Internet: "If the dollars per pupil were an accurate measure of performance, then the students in the District of Columbia should be among the best educated as they receive more money per pupil than almost any school district in the nation. However, when measured by standardized tests we find that their performance is among the worst. Conversely, the state of New Hampshire spends among the least on education and performs among the best. So let's be clear on something: you can't measure the quality of a school by the size of its budget."

There were other problems. One was that spending just wasn't making it to the students. Instead, it often ended up going to bureaucracy. Kansas City had been a famous landmark in the battle over segregation. So when a court ordered that the state pour money into Kansas City magnet schools in the hopes of making them the envy of the state, the nation watched. The school district spent $30 million a year busing students to the new magnet schools. It raised student funding up to $11,700 a pupil, almost double the national average. It provided the new schools with television and animation studios, a robotics lab, a zoo, and a model United Nations with simultaneous translation capabilities. People in other parts of Missouri were outraged at the court's decision, and even the judge who made the ruling was able to explain why. He told Paul Ciotti, an education writer who studied the matter for the Cato Institute, that "I had to balance two constitutional issues. One was no taxation without representation and the other was kids' right to an equal opportunity. I decided in favor of the schoolchildren."

But the result of the Kansas City experiment merely showed that trying to generate equality with money was a frustrating exercise. Computers stayed in crates on shelves until they were obsolete. The new inventory was so large that the school administrators lost track of it. Jay Nixon, the state attorney general, told Ciotti that at one time the district could not locate some twenty-three thousand items, including all the high-tech equipment and, at one moment, a baby grand piano. Yet student scores didn't improve. The prosperous families, most of them white, stayed away. Kansas City's schools stayed ghettos. Among the policy postmortems of the experiment was an important finding. To make their new system, the reformers had sacrificed local schools in the name of magnets. That had further weakened the schools, and the money just didn't compensate.

In Ohio, a state currently mired in an equalization battle, Governor George Voinovich has called for more spending to equalize schools. But Ohio has already spent quite a lot. The trouble is that money often doesn't go where it's supposed to go. When the state studied the matter it found that 50 percent of school money spent in Ohio never made it into the classroom.

The worst thing about the education battles is that they never seem to end. This is because, while every state court said that equality is important, every legislature has a different definition of *equal*. In some states, such as New Hampshire, *equal* meant fulfilling a minimum—the supreme court said "adequate." In other states, such as Vermont, it meant equal spending for everyone. The result was bitter quibbling that hasn't ended. In April 1998 *The New York Times* carried a feature story on the national scene. Its headline read PATCHWORK OF SCHOOL FINANCING SCHEMES OFFERS FEW ANSWERS AND MUCH CONFLICT. It reported that in New Mexico, decades after the state's original equalization change, districts and their attorneys were still fighting over cost-of-living adjustments, teacher salaries, and the education pie in general.

Across the nation, people had truly checked out. Total U.S. public expenditures per child have risen on average across the nation. But the increased spending is in part due to the fact that the baby boomers have long since passed through the schools: these days, there are fewer children in schools to spend the money on. And more money has not necessarily meant better students. Sam Peltzman, a scholar who looked at SAT scores, found a small statistical correlation between centralization and declines in SAT scores.

Nowhere was the price of the whole exercise clearer than in California. Nearly thirty years after *Serrano,* inflation has long subsided. Howard Jarvis and his famous results are footnotes in state history books. Yet California still spends less per pupil than many parts of the nation. The California failure was such a grand one that observers of all backgrounds could not help but note it. Decades after

Serrano Jonathan Kozol, an education writer who advocates equal spending, wrote in his book *Savage Inequalities* that although "the plaintiffs won the victory they sought, it was to some extent a victory of losers. Though the state ranks eighth in per capita income in the nation, the share of its income that now goes to public education is a meager 3.8 percent—placing California forty-sixth among the fifty states. Its average class size is the largest in the nation." He added with bitterness that "Beverly Hills still operates a high school that, in academic excellence, can rival those of Princeton and Winnetka. Baldwin Park still operates a poorly funded and inferior system." Nor did the rule of even distribution change student performance: Scholar Thomas Downes found that in terms of standardized-test scores, pupil performance didn't much change after equalization shifts.

Trying to Reconnect

The most compelling evidence of the Tiebout hypothesis, though, is not all the destruction it brought; it is that when towns and cities did try to reform their way out of the equalization method, it was always or nearly always through an effort to recapture the financing of their old local schools. Everywhere the accent was on striving to regain local control. Across the country, wherever possible, people try to find a way to reestablish the connection that centralization took away.

In California, parents developed their own method of getting around state control. They established local foundations—in effect, super PTA's—to serve their local schools through charity gifts from parents. By the mid-

1990s more than five hundred such foundations had formed, raising, together, some $30 million a year. The school that raised by far the most is a standout named Ross Elementary, in Marin County. The *San Francisco Examiner* reported that in 1998 almost 40 percent of the school's budget—more than $1 million—came from private money and a local tax. Its parents hosted a power benefit that auctioned off such goodies as a walk with Donald Trump in New York and a day watching director Barry Levinson while he worked.

In New York City the only parent movement to make the papers in years was an uprising at a school in Greenwich Village. A teacher was being laid off; the parents banded together and decided they would pay for a replacement. The city's school chancellor resisted; but after enormous public pressure, the parents were allowed to spend their money.

Wealthy and middle-class parents are not the only ones who feel the urge to control finances at their local school. In Georgia, Democrats have taken the lead in restoring the local connection. They allowed the counties to raise additional funds for school construction by voting for a county-level increase in sales tax. Within two years after a state amendment made it possible for them to fund this way, 129 counties—poor and rich—passed sales-tax increases for their schools. They raised a total of $3.5 billion. Because the result was local—they could see the buildings going up—people were happy to spend.

The nation's courts have frequently been hostile to school-voucher programs, which give families money back, or a credit, to spend on schools where they like. But families, in particular poor black families, like voucher arrangements very much. In Cleveland, Milwaukee, and New

York, they queue up to collect scholarships worth $2,000 or $3,000. The voucher arrangement doesn't really allow them to keep their tax money, sales tax, or property tax. Indeed, many poor families don't pay property tax at all because they don't own homes. But it restores to these people the local arrangement that has been lost. As such, vouchers are a sort of Jarvik heart of school finance: artificial, cumbersome, and exceptional, but the best thing available for the most desperate cases.

In an article entitled "School Reforms to Nowhere," syndicated columnist William Raspberry dismissed the centralized arrangement and laid out the case for a return to the local. Writing about Maryland's Prince George's County, he noted, "County Executive Wayne K. Curry, School Board Chair Alvin Thornton, and NAACP President Hardi L. Jones say they are looking forward to a future in which neighborhood schools, not mandatory busing, will be the salient feature. Neighborhood schools?! But that's what the (mostly white) opponents of busing were screaming for a quarter-century ago when the NAACP brought its desegregation suit. Neighborhood schools, the conventional wisdom then had it, was merely a code phrase for continued segregation. What has happened since then is that blacks have come into political ascendancy."

These results underline an important truth—something Mary Barrosse, and indeed almost every other parent, knows. It is that Chester Finn, the education scholar, was right: there is no limit to what people will spend on their children's education. But this holds only as long as the money they spend really goes to their children. Taking away that connection costs something. Directly or indirectly, it costs everyone, even those children on whose behalf the change was made. The lesson is clear: you can't fight for equity while ignoring taxation. If you do, you don't even get the equity you seek.

Over the winter following Act 60, Vermonters mounted a dramatic, desperate effort to recapture financial control of their children's education. The movement began in the state's very smallest towns. The parents of Winhall, a ski town, voted 4–1 to shut down their only public grammar school. They knew they would have to continue to send property taxes to Montpelier. But at least now the state would have little say in how they educated their children. They could use their $5,100 block grants as tuition at a new school, a private school they established. The block-grant money wasn't enough for a new school—indeed, it was only one seventh of the money the town was sending to Montpelier. But the parents decided they would raise the extra funds they needed by themselves and shut the state out.

Dover, a village with 719 voting souls, went another route. Voters there asked their selectpeople to take citizens' property-tax money and put it in escrow until Act 60 could be reviewed. Soon several other towns followed. "Our civil rebellion," one official deemed the tax revolt. By spring seven towns had planned or were seriously considering holding back their money. Dover officials were the feistiest. "They can't build a jail big enough," Marylou Raymo, the clerk of Dover, told *The Wall Street Journal.*

Other towns were, at least for the moment, more hesitant. Montpelier had an entire armory of laws, rules, and lawyers with which to strike back. It too could withhold funds, funds the towns counted on to maintain roads in icy winters. So they tried other avenues. In Dorset, locals met to ponder establishing a private charity to get around the high penalty they must pay if they wish to spend more through the public avenue. John Irving was so angry that he set about founding a private school, the Maple Street School, for his son and other disillusioned families. The school anticipated spending between $8,000 to $10,000 per child, or about the amount the town of Dorset was spending before equalization. The whole thing had made something of a cynic of him. He accused equalization's supporters of wrapping themselves in a mantle of equity. "It is easy to discriminate against a minority if that minority is allegedly well-to-do."

As for Mary Barrosse, her conclusion came to be that the whole story isn't about equity. "It has nothing to do with quality or equal education," she said. People wouldn't bother about paying property taxes, she knew, if they controlled those taxes to educate their children. Government might turn its back on that local connection, if it chose. It might choose to forget about individual parents and pursue statewide spending equity, school standards, national reading programs—whatever goal seemed important in the powerful, abstracted world of politics. But, as the Vermont school wars were proving, denying people a say also had its price.

8

YOUR ACCOUNTANT

TAX IS BIG BUSINESS, AND MANY AMERICAN COMPANIES spent July of 1997 watching the construction of that year's new tax law, the Taxpayer Relief Act of 1997. Perhaps no firm, though, followed what was being constructed in Washington as attentively as Young & Rubicam. A year earlier, the Chicago advertising firm had won the account of H&R Block, the nation's largest tax preparer, in a tense miniwar against four competitors. Now it had to prepare $15 million worth of commercials for the early weeks of the short tax season.

What sort of mood, the creative types wondered, would the big legislation engender? Washington legislators were presenting the law as good news that would cheer citizens: this was, after all, the first "net" tax cut—the first budget that aimed to cut the government's tax take—in a full decade. Perhaps the commercials ought to sell the tax breaks. But the law also had a downside. The 800 new amendments, 290 new sections, and 36 new retroactive provisions it added to the Internal Revenue Code were daunting. Maybe the campaign ought to do what the previous campaign had done—go negative, warn taxpayers about the new complexity, frighten viewers into seeking help.

By winter it was clear that fear had prevailed. The Young & Rubicam spots that showed up on television in January were tense ones, remarkably so when one considers that they aired in a country entering its eighth successive year of economic expansion. One commercial, labeled "Gobbledygook," featured a befuddled man trying to pull his tax documents together while a monotone voice in the background recited the changes in the tax code. As the man struggled, a second, soothing voice came on with reassuring talk about "experienced tax pros"—H&R Block. Then came the commercial's theme song, based on a Gershwin number: "Someone to Watch Over You."

Tax professionals wield extraordinary power in this country. We may not understand this when we are young, when our pay stubs and tax forms are simple and there seems no choice in the matter of taxes. But around about the middle of adulthood, as our tax lives become more complicated, as mortgage deductions, IRA's, 401(k)'s, and medical bills begin to crowd our financial calendars, we suddenly come to realize the nature of their might.

The first thing we understand is that these pencil people can help us save money. But we soon come to sense that there is something more important about them than the charm of savings that they bring us. We sense that we actually need these people. We need them for protection, even the near-godfather-style protection suggested in the Young & Rubicam ads. Americans often feel we owe the members of this odd trade even more than the $75, $200, $1,000, or $10,000 we pay them every year for handling our affairs. We pay them in bonuses in the form of tennis games, extra business, stock-market tips, even friendship. It's a debt born of desperation: "A dog who thinks he is man's best friend is a dog who obviously has never met a tax lawyer," says the writer Fran Lebowitz.

Sixty years ago this sort of humor was the stuff of *New Yorker* cartoons—taxes were a matter for the monied. But more recently, the cocktail set haven't been the only ones who turn to experts for help with their returns. By the fifties and sixties, the middle class had already begun seeking help with its 1040s. In the 1980s even the very lowest of earners, people who previously might never have had to file returns, turned ready and eager to pay fees to professionals for their services. Now, in the late 1990s, our national dependence has increased: in 1997 taxpayers who felt the need to turn to professional tax preparers numbered 58.9 million, a full half of all filers and the highest rate ever.

The sun in this modern tax firmament is H&R Block, a firm so big it prepares one in seven of all individual returns. In the spring of 1998 its chunky sans-serif typeface filled signs above 8,780 offices in fifty states. Walking down Main Street America, citizens are four times more likely to encounter an H&R Block office than they are to encounter the Gap. Its level of market penetration is the envy of every retail segment but fast food, and the talk of the New York Stock Exchange, where Block stock trades under the symbol HRB.

Block's disconcerting presence in our everyday lives tells us something about the nature of our struggle with the greedy hand. Unlike our forays into tax shopping, our income taxes are matters of gravity. This is partly true because of the power of the IRS, the most visible villain on the scene. With over 100,000 employees and a budget of $7.8

billion, the IRS is such a gorilla that it's no wonder people seek defenders against it. More important is the fact that the Internal Revenue Service actually has a statutory obligation to operate by spooking and threatening people. Our courts have reinforced that power. In the IRS regime, taxpayers are guilty until proven innocent, the opposite of the typical treatment for citizens by most of our authorities. In 1998 lawmakers made a big show of rectifying this with a new IRS law. The president signed the law at a desk over a telling sign reading PROTECTING AMERICAN TAXPAYERS AND THEIR VALUES. The new IRS law did restore some of citizens' rights in tax courts. But it did little to reduce the terror of the event many citizens fear most—the audit.

Everyone knows someone whom the IRS has audited. And we all know that we, too, are vulnerable to the authority's cruel reviews. Part of the fear here is the very randomness of the audit process. As a *Forbes* magazine author wrote, "The IRS has a new way to get ordinary, decent folks to comply with the tax code. Throw other, ordinary decent folks in jail." This is the reality of a system our laws still call "voluntary."

But the IRS, for all its damage, is not the true monster that Block grapples with. The true monster is the federal tax code itself. And the more complex it becomes, the harder it is for us to take on. These days the code has reached a level of complexity so widespread and so impermeable that we cannot figure out for ourselves how to escape the label "criminal." Even though the average rate of audits is down in recent years, we are less sure than ever that we can prepare the accurate return that will keep the demon away. We need the protectors—the tax doctors—to do that work for us.

The tax industry views this phenomenon the way a farmer views the weather—as a simple condition of business. The coming of the 1997 Taxpayer Relief Act, one of the most complicated tax laws on record, was described in the following way by Tom Field, editor of the tax world's preeminent periodical, *Tax Notes:* "The passage of the 1997 Act marked a bright and happy day for any tax preparer, tax adviser, or tax publisher." H&R Block's Kansas City headquarters also reacted with excitement to the act. "This bill creates the most relief and causes the most confusion," burbled an October press release, before detailing the eleven rates the law visited on capital gains.

Reached by phone in Kansas City, Henry Bloch, the firm's seventy-five-year-old founder, offered some thoughts on the matter. "Every year a few more people throw up their hands and say, 'I can't prepare my return anymore,' " he said. "Every time government changes things, business does increase." More complex changes mean more business for tax experts. Call it Bloch's law.

The fortunes of H&R Block are worth tracing a little further back than the 1990s, if only because they demonstrate how Bloch's law came to play such a role in our lives. In the 1930s, there was no H&R Block, because for most Americans there was no income tax. There were only two brothers, Henry and Richard Bloch, who worked as professional bookkeepers. Tax preparers as we know them today did not exist.

This of course is not to say that those who did have to complete the Form 1040 found it easy going. One of the more memorable samples of such a forlorn figure sits in the Franklin D. Roosevelt Library—a plea for help to the commissioner of Internal Revenue from FDR himself. An

unsigned copy of the March 15, 1938, item is worth reprint-
ing in its entirety, if only because of the familiar tax confusion that it conveys:

My dear Commissioner Helvering:

I am enclosing my income tax return for the calendar year 1937, together with my check for $15,000.

I am wholly unable to figure out the amount of
the tax for the following reason:

The first twenty days of January, 1937, were a
part of my first term of office and to these twenty
days the income tax rates as of March 4, 1933 apply.
To the other 345 days of the year 1937, the income
tax rates as they existed on January 30, 1937 apply.

As this is a problem in higher mathematics, may
I ask that the Bureau let me know the amount of the
balance due? The payment of $15,000 doubtless
represents a good deal more than half what the
eventual tax will prove to be.

World War II brought the Bloch brothers their grand opportunity: many Americans were now, for the first time, filing returns, and like FDR, they were finding the affair a
daunting one. The Bloch brothers saw that their business
clients also wanted help preparing individual returns. They
founded their firm in 1955, picking an easier spelling
for its name—Block. (The corporation reports that they
feared people might pronounce their name "blotch" if they
didn't change the spelling.) The brothers charged $5 per
return.

The astral rates and numerous deductions that characterized the tax code in the 1950s made Block an instant hit. In 1955, recalls Henry Bloch, "the top marginal rate on the income tax was 91 percent, so getting a deduction right meant that a "one-dollar gift to charity cost the taxpayer only nine cents." By 1969, with the top tax rate still an impressive 77 percent, three thousand Block offices dotted the continent. In the seventies the winds of inflation blew many Americans into higher and higher tax brackets—the famous bracket creep. They too turned to Block.

All the "reforms" of the 1960s, 1970s, and 1980s brought yet more business for Block. To be sure, tax rates were sometimes lower than they had been before. But the rules changed more and more frequently. "Change is good for tax preparers" is an important corollary of Bloch's law. The trend of accelerating change unnerved Americans and widened their dependence on tax preparers yet again. Block founded a successful tax school to train tax preparers for seasonal work; today that school teaches tens of thousands. The textbooks it produces on the code are widely admired as among the best in the field—even by civil servants within the IRS. The heft of the company's consumer handbook to tax, issued annually, provides another measure of the code's growing complexity. When the *H&R Block Income Tax Guide* was first published in the 1960s, it had 196 pages. By 1988 it was up to 317 pages; in 1998 its pages numbered 574.

Notice that we are talking about H&R Block here—not Deloitte & Touche or Arthur Andersen, which grew to be giants in the same period for other reasons. Block's rise, at least in the 1980s and 1990s, was the result of a new and intense preoccupation of lawmakers: fiddling with the end of the tax code that affected lower earners. The arrival of the Earned Income Credit, a giant rebate program, changed the nature of tax preparers like Block or Jackson Hewitt. It shifted their occupation from that of pencil-pushing expert toward that of credit officer, or loan shark. Today, Block and Jackson Hewitt customers often claim the credit. Block wires their claim to the IRS, which in turn checks with the Social Security Administration to verify their entitlement.

Today Block is so big that the federal government relies on the firm to get through the blizzard of 120 million individual returns filed each year, a fact that even the highest of tax authorities acknowledge. "We were utterly dependent on them to make the system work," Fred Goldberg, an IRS commissioner in the Bush years, recalled. "And they were wonderful." His comment is, in its way, a frightening one. It suggests that taxpayers may be certain where government begins—with the tax law. But they cannot always be sure where it ends.

And Block is merely the most visible symbol of the modern traffic in anxiety. Two other chains that prepare individual returns, Jackson Hewitt and Gilman & Ciocia, are so large that their stock is publicly traded. To them add an army of individual tax preparers who simply hang out their shingle in tax season. The infantry speak with breathless respect of tax preparers who carry the mysterious initials "E.A." after their names. "E.A." stands for "enrolled agent," the rank given to those who have the privilege of representing clients before the IRS in tax court. These are the gladiators among the tax preparers, the front-line fighters who go hand to hand with the IRS henchmen.

Then, higher up, come the tens of thousands of certified public accountants who prepare returns for businesses or work in the auditing side of the field. They also may appear in tax court. Finally come the elite of the tax business—the tax attorneys, a highly paid, wing-tip crowd, largely male. As one tax attorney said, "The tax bar is commonly referred to as a 'special priesthood,' and it is only slightly more tolerant than the Catholic Church in ordaining women tax priests." All told, Americans pay something like $40 billion a year to the tax clerisy for tax counsel, advice, or protection of some sort.

Our tax protectors are generally good to us. After all, it is we who pay them. Still, the nature of their work has generated a wealth of humor. Many of these jokes are just rewrites of bad jokes from other much derided trades: "What do you call a thousand accountants at the bottom of the ocean?" "A good start." But some are quite specific to the tax trade. "What's the difference between the short and long income tax forms?" "If you use the short form, the government gets your money. If you use the long form, the accountant gets it." Others seek to diminish tax experts' talent by belittling the product of their work: "What's the definition of a good tax accountant?" "Someone who has a loophole named after him." Another favorite: "How do you torture an accountant?" "Tie him to his chair and then fold a map up wrong in front of him."

What the jokes reflect is that while Americans need accountants, we resent them too. They are evidence of our weakness in the face of the greedy hand: even though we would rather wage this battle ourselves, we end up turning to the tax men to help us. At times too these fellows seem less advocates and more good cops whose charm lies in the fact that they are better than the bad cop—the IRS.

There's actually a certain legitimacy to this suspicion.

Unlike other advocates, tax experts, particularly personal accountants and enrolled agents, don't stand before a different judge in a different court every time they argue for a client. They labor in the purgatory of administrative law. Most of their cases are heard in the same place, tax court. And unlike other advocates, tax experts don't have a different opponent every time they go to trial. Their opponent is almost always the same—the IRS. And that IRS is not just any opponent, it is the one—in the enrolled agents' case at least—that certified them in the first place. It knows them and knows that they have cosigned the returns they prepared. Rejection by the IRS can be the end of a tax preparer's career. Tax preparers and accountants don't enjoy anything like the attorney-client privilege that is the tradition in the law. That's why wealthy people with tax problems invariably hire an attorney.

Even without this legal difference, though, many of the tax doctors would still end up taking the government's side. They have learned, over the course of their careers, that it is better to side with an immutable power than with transient, fickle clientele. In fact, the tax-preparation trade is so vulnerable to the IRS and to the rigors of the tax code that it *attracts* people who don't mind handing down bad news or being government's servants. In the established diagnostic tests that type personality for career planning, accountants don't show up in the same category as economists, lawyers, or congressmen, three other fields that have plenty to do with tax. They fall into what some of these tests call the "duty" category, which attracts law enforcers, good guys, order keepers, and nitpickers. "Accountants hate change," says Carla Rollandini, an expert in the Myers-Briggs Type

Indicator, the most famous of these personality tests. "And they like to be right." In other words, the same thing that we love in our accountants—their exactitude—is also the thing that disappoints us and, at times, drives us nuts. They play Felix to our Oscar. In the paradigm of career types that Rollandini hands out to clients, the accountant falls into the same category as the mortician.

There's one positive aspect to all the gloom caused by tax complexity. It is possible for the average man to make money off it. In 1997, as the damage of the new tax law became clear, Wall Street demonstrated its faith in Bloch's law in dramatic fashion. It bought up millions of shares in the nation's tax preparers. Brian Wesbury, an economist with a Chicago bond house, actually created a special Index of Complexity, made of the stock of the three publicly traded tax preparers. Wesbury tracked his index from the day House Ways and Means chairman Bill Archer and the White House started signaling that they were close to a budget deal, and through the course of an autumn when Wall Street and Main Street alike were discovering hidden confusions in the new tax law. By Christmas, or half a year later, the Complexity Index had risen an astounding 250 percent, a rate that dwarfed the Standard & Poors 500, the Nasdaq, and the Dow Jones Industrial Average in one of those indexes' best half years on record.

Given such power, one would expect the tax-preparation lobby to be one of the biggest amphibians to walk Washington's Gucci Gulch. Yet tax preparers don't do anything like the turbo-lobbying one sees from the real estate industry, the telecom industry, or the American Association of Retired Persons. Perhaps this is so because they perceive that the trend is moving in their direction anyway. "Tax professionals are just about the only Americans who do not complain about the complexity of our tax laws," wrote Larry Elkin, a financial planner, in a note to colleagues on his Web site. "After all, if mere commoners could find their fiscal fortunes in the Internal Revenue Code, how would oracles like us ever command $400 an hour?"

Lately, though, as tax law has become so very complex, observers can sense tension in the tax field, the tension being over whether the code is testing the limits of even the tax brains. To put it in the terms of one of the accounting jokes, Congress these days regularly folds up maps wrong before accountants' eyes. Lawmakers change laws so very frequently, attaching new vagaries to old ones, that their pencil work is rendered a fiction.

Every year *Money* magazine dramatizes this situation with a famous test. It picks a sample tax return and asks tax preparers to volunteer to prepare it. Every year dozens of tax preparers do. And every year they fall on their swords. In 1997 forty-five brave individuals, professional tax hands all, dared to prepare *Money*'s sample return. They came out with forty-five different bottom lines—and none of them were right. "Fewer than one in four came within $1,000 of the correct answer," commented *Money*. The tax preparers looked to be as duped as their clients.

These new humiliations have cast something of a shadow over the lives of accountants and other tax doctors. They are a people who have been betrayed by their own discipline. In the mid-1990s, frustration over the code actually drove a brave Connecticut accountant named Theodore Krauss to rebel. He started a small nonprofit group whose very name might seem an oxymoron: Accountants for Tax Reform.

This frustration is visible even in the ultimate tax people, the IRS civil servants themselves. In the spring of 1998 I called on a high-ranking officer whose official title was taxpayer advocate. He was a loyal IRS employee who had served the institution thirty-two years, climbing from the rank of GS-4 to GS-14 all the way up into various grades of executive bureaucrat. His job as advocate allowed him to intervene in individual cases when he felt like it, a prerogative that gave him a power to determine personal fates that was something akin to that of an inquisitor in the Spain of Ferdinand and Isabella.

Yet this inquisitor—his name is Lee Monks—was not serene. Congress had created his position in order to flag and halt the most flagrant IRS abuses. It had recently asked him to come up with some solutions to various IRS problems. These ranged from the simple to the compelling to the ridiculous. One bugaboo he found, for example, was known as the "rounding problem": taxpayers who chose not to round the numbers on their returns to the nearest dollar were making errors and incurring penalties. The inquisitor recommended mandatory rounding.

The most alarming and saddest of the challenges faced by this green-eye-shade figure was mentioned in Item 15 in a long list of recommendations for change he had made to the federal government: "suicide threats." His memo relayed, *en passant,* a horrifying little fact: that taxpayers have threatened suicide "as part of a tax-related issue." Under the IRS attorneys' broad interpretation of confidentiality laws, IRS agents faced with suicide threats from desperate filers were not allowed to pick up the phone and call the local police. The taxpayer advocate pleaded for the authority to snip through its own red tape for these cases, just once: "the potential to save a human life clearly overshadows other concerns in this area." Soon afterward, lawmakers got to work changing the suicide problem with the IRS-reform law.

But the taxpayer advocate was quite frank about conceding that IRS reform had its limits and that his projects were really mere Band-Aids. "We could give you five or more ideas of how to fix the IRS, but that is piecemeal work," he said. The real problem, he admitted, was indeed the code itself. "In essence," he added, small tax changes weren't worth much. Unless you change the whole system, "you get nowhere."

Such moments of introspection are rare. And, after all, why should one expect otherwise? Self-destructive statements are bad for business. It is simply not in the tax people's interest to make them. At least not if there's so much money to be made when the trade stays in denial.

In the fall of 1997, when I first contacted H&R Block headquarters to talk about how the most complex tax law in years would affect the firm's bottom line, its media staff didn't like it. Wary that the press would present them as profiteers living off Americans' tax troubles, they went to elaborate length to stress other aspects of their business—a new auto-insurance program and a product for the very long term that bore the quaint label "will kit."

By the new year, when it became clear what a bonanza the new tax law would yield, the Block staff stopped steering me away from the topic. And when I called Block again in March—at the high point of tax season—their spokes-woman was in too good a mood to worry about elaborate refutations. In the sixty-odd days since we had last spoken, Block and its franchises had raked in $685 million from tax-payers in exchange for preparing and filing their returns. Of course, she allowed, it was true that a complex code was good for the industry. She was a polite woman doing her job, but her manner conveyed hurry, and one could not help but have sympathy for her impatience. Who, after all, had time to parse or confirm theory, when volume was up 10 percent?

9

YOUR SUCCESS

IN AUGUST 1966 GEORGE HARRISON LED THE ALBUM *Revolver* with a song about a new presence in his life— "Taxman." The lyrics were very simple. "Let me tell you how it will be. There's one for you, nineteen for me. 'Cos I'm the taxman."

It was no accident that "Taxman" appeared on *Revolver* and not *Please, Please Me*. That early LP was released when the Beatles still thought of themselves as Liverpool nightclub boys whose flame might go out as suddenly as it had ignited. *Abbey Road* came too late. By then the Beatles were dulled to their own success.

In truth, 1966 was exactly the right time for the Beatles to discover "Taxman." This was the period when they were just settling in to the notion of their stupendous success. In the Britain of the 1960s that meant they were taxed like lords and dukes, at confiscatory rates ranging far above half their incomes. No matter how much they earned, and they were earning far more than they had ever dreamed, it seemed the government took more. "Taxman" even makes specific reference to the confiscators, Mr. Wilson and Mr.

Heath, British politicians from the period whose names must puzzle the curious twelve-year-olds who pull out their parents' old records and cassettes for an afternoon rumpus in the living room.

Older Americans may no longer identify quite so much with the Beatles' music. But they can identify, more than ever, with the younger George's shock. This is because, in some way or another, we are all Beatles now: people in the process of achieving more than we once thought we could. With our achievement comes the George Harrison experience. Suddenly we—little me!—are paying taxes in the 30, 40, even 50 percent range. Even if we aren't yet confronting such rates, we are aware that our work may soon get us to that territory. We look around, stunned, for we don't really *feel* rich. In fact, we may feel tired, because we have been working harder than ever to make the progress we've made. So we wonder: why is it that my effort earns a bonus from my employer and punishment from my government? Indeed, in other, bumpier years, the code did not punish us in quite the way it does now.

Not that this internal dialogue changes things. Today we are rich, at least in the eyes of the tax man. Our newfound prosperity is, to use Paine's phrase, the greedy hand's most deserved "prey."

This is a fundamental moment in our relationship with our government. When we struggle with taxes that come with our new prosperity—call them "success taxes"—we are struggling not with some peripheral tax pitfall but with the core principle of the code—progressivity. Progressivity is a success tax, but it is also the mother of all taxes, the tax that dominates our lives like no other. Progressivity institutionalizes the class warfare that politicians tell us they are waging on our behalf.

Yet progressivity is not an intuitive thing: as we look at our tax bills, we find we are forced to explain to ourselves exactly how it works. Many of us simply fall back to assuming that progressivity is what makes rich people pay more taxes. That's not right. When the tax rate is 25 percent, a person who earns $100 pays $25. A person who earns $200 pays more. He pays $50. That's called a proportionate system, and it is not what we have.

What we have is progressivity, a system that taxes people more the higher up the income scale they go. Our first dollars are taxed at lower rates: nothing at all, or 15 or 20 percent. But the last dollar we earn is taxed at higher rates, rates that, on the federal level, currently range up to 39.6 percent. Medicare drives that rate up to 40.6. Some states push that figure toward 50 percent by applying their own progressive tax structure. We encounter the progressivity problem at many points in our lives: progressivity is at the heart of the marriage penalty, for example. But only with significant achievement, only when we actually come close to managing the seemingly Herculean feat of actually doing in life what we set out to do, do we move up the tax brackets toward the 39.6, or 45, or 50 percent zenith; only then do we begin to know progressivity's full damage.

Today Washington talks as if progressivity were etched in stone—no reform plan, not even the intrepid flat taxers', dares offer a program totally devoid of progressive elements. Many politicians play on progressivity's very name and act as if attacking progressivity is attacking progress itself. Yet, when pollsters ask Americans how they feel about progressivity, different answers emerge. In 1995, for example, *Reader's*

Digest published the results of a poll by Everett Ladd, a professor of political science and director of the Roper Center for Public Opinion Research at the University of Connecticut. The Roper poll showed that a broad majority of people felt that 25 percent was about the share of their money Americans should pay in all their taxes. It also showed that Americans earning less than $30,000 agreed, along with all other earners, that 25 percent should be the top tax burden for families with incomes of $200,000. That's well below the average taxes many such families actually confront.

What those laboring in the trenches of everyday life have sensed is that progressivity doesn't do what it says it does: tax the rich. Indeed, the secret of progressivity, and all the other little success taxes we have constructed over time, is that they aren't really success taxes. They are taxes on *becoming successful*, or merely improving one's lot. Those who are truly successful, the superrich, get to stay that way and even build their wealth. Those who aren't, or aren't yet, get the following message: stay where you are. When you move upward, you will start to lose a lot of breaks that are valuable to you.

Here's the way the progressivity trap works. Progressivity makes the tax rate on what accountants call "ordinary income" very high. So the superrich, and even people who are merely very prosperous, arrange to get deferred-compensation plans that will pay them in years when their taxes are lower.

Or they take their money in stock and stock options, which will be taxed, at least in part, at the lower rates that apply to capital gains. One of the most famous examples of a high earner to do this was the tennis star Andre Agassi, who took stock options as part of a deal with Nike; when that stock quadrupled the following year, he made money on the stock's rise—on top of any tax savings.

Far lesser names than Agassi profit from similar deals on their company options. They can afford to hold on to company stock they are offered. So they exercise their options early and pay income tax on the rise in the stock that has occurred since the options were issued. Then they hold on to the stock and watch it rise some more. That share of the rise is treated as a capital gain. The wealthier they are, the longer they can afford to hold on to the stock, and the lower the average tax rate they pay on their options arrangement. The same category even gets a break on a success tax that whams the rest of us from time to time, the alternative minimum tax, or AMT. The AMT was designed expressly for the rich. But it often ends up being a tax *break* for them, since its 28 percent rate is well below their statutory top income tax rate, 39.6 percent.

But what about the the poor souls who need to pay for college or housing and so exercise their options the moment they get them? They cannot afford to buy the stock and then hold on to it. If they exercise an option to buy their company stock at $20 at a moment when it is selling for $40, they must treat the entire $20 difference as ordinary income, taxed at a higher rate. Often, *all* the income Americans make on their options, therefore, is subject to progressivity. They pay the highest taxes of anyone on their option rewards.

Americans do recognize what is going on, although they are not always able to articulate it. And they resent it. The resentment runs so deep that whenever a very wealthy man gets caught in the IRS's net, they relish the spectacle. When the IRS sued Leona Helmsley, the wife of hotel mogul Harry Helmsley, for disguising renovations to her Greenwich, Connecticut, mansion as business expenses, her boxy face graced the tabloids for months. By far the best-remembered line from the case was one reported by her maid in Greenwich. Mrs. Helmsley, the maid testified, had told her that people like the Helmsleys didn't pay taxes; "only the little people pay taxes." The quote infuriated people, principally for its arrogance. But newspaper readers were also angry for another reason: they sensed that Leona had spoken the truth.

Fatal Illusion

How America, land of strivers, came to target those strivers like so many Iraqi chemical-weapons factories is an instructive story. Certainly, the nation's founders never advocated "success taxes." Thomas Jefferson ran for office in 1799 on a plan to ban all internal taxes—and won. One of Jefferson's most famous promises was that a "wise and frugal government" would not "take from the mouth of labor the bread it has earned." Andrew Jackson, the father of the Democratic party, also abhorred taking away from the small, individual achiever, and the America of the half century that followed was truly a Jacksonian place, the place of Tocqueville's "self-interest, rightly understood."

Every time the nation's leaders doubted their convictions, they had only to look at Europe. There numerous success taxes and big, rigid governments killed enterprise and dampened free spirits. Tocqueville, a French nobleman whose family had barely made it through the French Revolution, knew all too well what damage could be wrought in the name of punishing the wealthy. In the same years that he was traveling in America, one of his more gifted countrymen, the economist Frederic Bastiat, unfurled perhaps the best explanation ever on why governments favor success taxes. Lower earners who would not normally tolerate a tax, Bastiat noted, will tolerate one when they believe that the rich are being taxed even more. "People are beginning to realize that the apparatus of government is costly. But what they do not know is that the burden falls *inevitably* on them. They have been led to believe that if their share has been heavy until now the Republic has a means, while increasing the general burden, of shifting at least the larger part of it onto the shoulders of the rich. Fatal Illusion!"

Fifty years after Bastiat sketched it, most Americans still understood the danger of his fatal illusion. It was still bedrock American principle that people be able to keep the fruits of their own labor. Bourke Cockran, the Democratic leader in the House of Representatives before the turn of the century, thought that installing a progressive tax was a terrible plan. He noted such a tax would fall heavily on a crucial group: younger people starting out, first-generation arrivals, average Americans who might have little but who hoped to one day make a success of their lives. "The hope of wealth, which is universal, is a greater force for order than the possession of wealth, which is confined to a few." In those years William Jennings Bryan campaigned on a Democratic-party platform that explicitly rejected progressivity. The platform said, "We favor an income tax as part of our income . . . to the end that wealth may bear its proportionate share of the burdens of the federal government."

As has often been the case in our history, the Republicans ended up doing the dirty work. The Republican leadership in the House and Senate, and a Republican president, Taft, were the ones who began the institutionalization of class warfare. When they wrote the Sixteenth Amendment, the law that gave us the income tax, the Republicans went where the Democratic party had refused to go. Their amendment said that "Congress shall have power to lay and collect taxes on incomes, from whatever source derived." This left the door open for progressivity and the income tax.

Scholars today often wonder whether the Republicans actually realized what they were setting in motion. Theirs was supposed to be a levy on the wealthy. When it did come, the new income tax, passed by a Democratic Congress in 1913 as part of the Underwood-Simmons Tariff Act, exempted all but two in a hundred of American households. Its top rate was 7 percent, less than what individuals pay today for their share of payroll taxes. It is fair to say none of the Republicans who laid the grounds for progressivity ever dreamed of income tax rates at 39.6 percent. In fact, there was a floor debate at the time on whether to put a 10 percent cap in the constitutional amendment. The answer was no—largely because people thought the idea that the tax might ever rise that high too absurd to address. This was a success tax that might, in the words of the Philadelphia *Public Ledger,* "mulct the wealthy"; but it would "mulct" them moderately, and it would leave the rest of the country alone.

But within a few very short years—the years that brought World War I—the first of these promises already lay broken. The Wilson administration didn't just take something from the wealthy; it pushed top rates on the income tax up to 67 percent. It also loaded on corporate-profits taxes—so-called "excess profits" taxes—of up to 60 percent. Progressivity was crucial to FDR's mass tax. FDR made a big show of taxing the wealthy. And so, in the 1940s, average people began to pay taxes, including the success taxes of progressivity. They did so in part because they could promise that wealthier people were paying yet higher success taxes. Bastiat's fatal illusion was up and running in the United States.

Government liked the fatal illusion. "We shall tax and tax, and spend and spend, and elect and elect," said Roosevelt's adviser Harry Hopkins in a merry moment. Federal tax revenues jumped by tens of billions. By the Korean War the government's collection from income and profits taxes was $50 billion, more than twenty-five times what it had been in 1940. There were those who questioned progressivity. J. K. Lasser, the renowned tax-guide guru, published an angry article in the *Atlantic Monthly* headlined "Confiscatory." But most economic thinkers and politicians, from left to right, embraced it. Even the most famous of the right-wing eminences, the Austrian economist Friedrich von Hayek, endorsed a progressive rate structure in those years, allowing that "some progression of the direct taxes may not only be permissible but necessary to offset the tendency of indirect taxes to be regressive."

Yet even in the 1940s and 1950s, what we know today was clear: the class-warfare part of progressivity didn't really function as advertised. In the 1940s and 1950s most Americans were paying progressive taxes for the first time. They consoled themselves with the knowledge that the nation's wealthy were paying the highest taxes in U.S. history. At one point the top marginal rate on the income tax was 91 percent. Even then, though, the rich had found a way to evade these taxes. They asked Washington for tickets out of this regime, and Washington handed out those tickets by inserting tiny favors to specific groups into the tax code. There was the family-partnership trick: the more partners a family could find for its business, the lower its effective tax rate. Families took advantage of this by making their own children partners. Hence the following amusing dialogue from a court case involving partners ages seven, five, two, and three months, culled by the journalist Philip Stern for his book *The Great Treasury Raid:*

> Court to wife: Now do you participate in the
>   management of the business of the La Salle
>   Livestock Company?
> A: Well, I have been producing partners.
> Q: Beg pardon?
> A: I have been too busy producing partners so far.

Progressivity made these years the heyday of the loophole—an era of legal and near-legal Leona Helmsley–esque ploys. The capital-gains rates were much lower than the income tax, and an elite class of business executives at firms from U.S. Steel to Celanese to American Airlines to Sears, Roebuck avoided the success penalties of the income tax by taking stock options. Special tax breaks, the famous depletions, enabled one oil multimillionaire to pay no tax for more than a decade. Louis B. Mayer was spared $2 million in taxes when Congress created a special tax provision just for him: Section 1240 of the 1954 Internal Revenue Code. The period also had its share of true lawbreakers, some of them abetted by officials at the Bureau of Internal Revenue. The federal tax-collection organ was found to be so corrupt that Congress held hearings and gave the agency the name we know today: Internal Revenue Service.

In the 1960s, ordinary Americans continued to pay success taxes—top rates came down, but not much—and the rich *still* avoided them. This was something wealthy people saw as a basic fact of life but that the more idealistic media, who covered the lives of the wealthy, often failed to perceive. The business writer John Brooks described the awakening of the television host, David Susskind: "On television one evening in middle 1960s, David Susskind asked six assembled multimillionaries whether any of them considered tax rates a stumbling block on the high road to wealth in America. There was a long silence, almost as if the notion were new to the multimillionaires, and then one of them, in the tone of someone explaining something to a child, mentioned the capital gains provision and said that he didn't consider taxes much of a problem. There was no more discussion of high tax rates that night."

Eventually, people began to see through the fatal illusion. A Treasury Department study released in January 1969 revealed an outrageous fact: 155 people making more than $200,000 had paid no federal income tax. That's the equivalent of closer to a million in 1997. So Congress came up with a new success tax that, it promised, would do better at punishing the plutocrats. They created a "rich guy tax," the precursor to today's alternative minimum tax.

To stop the bad guys from getting away with their oil depletions, mink farms, and other tax deductions, lawmakers constructed a separate tax system, with its own exemptions and rates but very few deductions. Even if a taxpayer's return looked fine within the context of the ordinary code, it very often flunked the AMT test. If he had relatively numerous deductions compared with income, he had to pay the AMT or his regular tax bill, whichever was higher. The AMT purgatory was not a place anyone went to voluntarily.

Yet again, the success tax backfired. Today, many people far less wealthy than the fat cats who were the AMT's original targets find themselves in AMT purgatory. Indeed, the AMT hits many who earn well under $100,000. That is because the AMT exemption amount has not been raised to adjust for inflation over the years. Some of the victims are mothers claiming dependent-care credits; others are those claiming large medical deductions. Those with a good accountant or even TurboTax may be able to avoid the trick; the computer program, for example, even announces this advantage: "Luckily," a lady in a little box tells the reader, "the program automatically locates most of the deductions and income items that will trigger the AMT."

And since the AMT program, like progressivity, is supposed to be for "higher-income" people, it catches humbler taxpayers by surprise. Since most of these people count on the deductions that have triggered the AMT, that surprise is a bitter one. Ann Wengler, a divorced developmental psychologist, was one such victim. *Forbes* magazine, which told her story, reported that she had four children to raise but wasn't able to get any of the child credits Congress worked to establish for families, even though her adjusted gross income was around $58,000. Her other credits trigger the AMT—in the eyes of our tax code, she was rich.

Another AMT casualty is Norman Earl Holly, a retired government economist. Holly was a few years away from his pension when he got into a dispute at his office at the U.S. Public Health Service. He resigned in anger, and filed a grievance with the government against his office. The legal costs were $30,247 in one year. His adjusted gross income was $49,379, hardly anyone's definition of wealthy—not even Congress's. So he deducted the expense of the legal bill, along with a few other, minor items. As it happens, the code is uncharacteristically gracious when it comes to lawsuits that involve defamation, Holly's claim. It allows deductions for them, under the principle that what hurts a person's reputation also hurts his pocketbook—certainly a useful little position in these litigious days. In any case, the IRS didn't dispute the legitimacy of Holly's deduction.

Instead, though, the IRS had another problem. It said that Holly was taking *too many* deductions for its liking. This even though Holly's accountant, a volunteer tax preparer personally supervised by the IRS, had never brought up the matter. Holly's tax bill, the IRS told him years later, must be reestimated under the AMT regime. The IRS decided he owed $3,000 extra, plus a penalty.

Holly, who was turning seventy, had had some brushes with the IRS before. He had been audited six times in a single decade. Three of those audits had actually resulted in refunds to him, and the other three got "no change" determinations. So he decided to argue his own case in tax court. His position was simple. Congress had said expressly that the AMT was not for people like him. And Holly, a retiree who drove a ten-year-old Toyota Corolla, was hardly a fat cat. Nowhere in laws that they had written did they say people earning $50,000 should pay the AMT. Why should he pay a tax designed for the wealthy? That argument didn't sell the judge. If the statutes said someone in this category had to pay the AMT, he had to pay it. Indeed, the judge commented that the bureaucracy was just doing its job. "Although the results may seem harsh to petitioner in this case, Congress created the AMT by enacting the applicable statutory provisions, and we do not have the authority to disregard a legislative mandate." In other words, the judge did what administrative judges almost always do. He said, "This isn't my problem." Holly had to pay.

AMT Epidemic

Gary and Aldona Robbins, two economists who have produced the best study laying out the problem, note that the AMT hurts our general welfare because it is what economists call "countercyclical." The AMT strikes when the amount of deductions to regular income looks particularly high. In poor years—during recessions—businesses are in exactly that situation: they have relatively high deductions and relatively low income. So the moment when businesses are most vulnerable is the moment when they are most likely to face the higher taxes of the AMT trap. Long ago, with the start of the Depression, Americans learned that raising taxes as you go into a recession is a terrible thing to do. More recently Japan too has shown us what damage that can do. Yet that is exactly what the AMT's effect is on our businesses, causing them to downsize, lay off, and otherwise punish the average person.

Critics of this argument point out that the AMT is merely a small bugaboo. The IRS estimates that it hits fewer than 1 in 150 taxpayers. Indeed, the AMT is a pretty inefficient tax. It costs $1.5 billion to collect, or about the value of a third of the revenue it brings in.

In the future, though, more and more citizens will come to know this painful gizmo. In fewer than ten years, unless Congress indexes the exemption, the AMT trap will close on nine million taxpayers—one out of fourteen. As their wages move up, people move into the category where they are subject to this tax. Many of these people will be taxpayers with between $50,000 and $100,000 in adjusted gross income. Corporations will also find themselves increasingly subject to the AMT. At *The Wall Street Journal,* we editors titled an editorial about this "AMT Cash Machine."

There are other little success taxes that penalize people for trying to make something of their lives. Some are taxes on enterprise. Yes, enterprise! Since the downsizing of the early 1990s, everyone in America but the ostriches knows that the most dangerous thing in the world is to assume that their corporation will take care of them, like some loving daddy, until retirement. It has become clear that the only way to survive is to break out and somehow build a franchise of one's own, so that when the day of downsizing comes we will be ready.

"Prepare for Audit Strikes"

Yet the tax code and its soldiers, IRS agents, regularly persecute tiny entrepreneurial efforts, so that starting a business often means entering a minefield. The persecution starts with the very first step, setting up a home business. To deduct the cost of a business telephone, it forces people to set up a separate line. To deduct the cost of a computer we use for business at home, we must follow a complicated set of rules. Then there is the problem of independent contractors.

The IRS audits people with small businesses far more frequently than it does those who choose to be employed by someone else. By now, the nation's entrepreneurs are forced into a sort of bunker mentality. "There is one predominant, ever watchful adversary (enemy) of every self-employed individual. Said adversary is government," writes Holmes F. Crouch, the author of a vehement little handbook, *Being Self-Employed: Prepare for IRS Surveillance & Audit Strikes.* Crouch adds, "Within five to ten years after being self-employed, we can virtually guarantee that we will be after you with fang and tong." This sounds a tad paranoid, but audit rates confirm it. Crouch points out that the audits are particularly likely to strike when income goes above $100,000—in other words, when the independent contractor is beginning to succeed.

Some independent businesses face extra tax hazards. Everyone from Steve Forbes to Al Gore has lauded Americans who start their own high-tech businesses and make it in this much admired sector. The lone computer programmer has come to symbolize that success: he is to this age what the engineer was to the era of the railroads, or the farmer to the frontier. Vice President Gore is so proud of these successes that he regularly meets with a group of entrepreneurs in a special club the media has dubbed "Gore-Tech." He also recently took Viktor Chernomyrdin, the Russian politician, on a personal tour of Silicon Valley to meet that American phenomenon, the individual entrepreneur.

But success taxes treat this American paragon like a pariah. Under a recent law, the IRS persecutes companies who hire computer programmers as independent contractors. It makes hiring an independent contractor—as opposed to an employee—an invitation to trouble. "Who do you know who would hire someone who will bring with them trouble from the IRS?" Harvey J. Shulman, the lawyer for the national Association of Computer Consultant Businesses, asked *The New York Times.*

This law was passed by a Congress that thought it could cattle-prod more independent types into working as regular employees, who are easier to collect taxes from than independent businesses. The IRS didn't write the law, but one can guess it takes some pleasure in enforcing it. Employees *are* easier to tax than independents. After it was passed, people who backed the law tried to reverse it. But reversing something in Washington isn't always easy, and at this writing the independent-programmer item is still on the books.

Then there are the little success punishments that aren't even classed as taxes. One of the most important of all is, surprisingly, financial aid for college. Our government and our nation's universities spend billions every year financing the educations of "needy students." But when people stop being "needy," their parents have to pay full tuition. That makes saving for college very expensive, particularly for people whose household income and savings are right around the edge of the financial-aid limits. For every dollar they put away, they lose a dollar in financial aid. This is a 100 percent success tax, a success tax on savings.

Justifying the Success Taxes

Over the years Washington, eager to maintain its fatal illusion, has come up with any number of justifications for its success taxes. After World War II the foremost of these was something that seems surprising today: inflation. In the thinking of the Keynesians, high taxes were necessary even after World War II had ended, in order to restrain inflation. Keynes himself, far cleverer than any Keynesian, was to say that "the avoidance of taxes is the only intellectual pursuit that still carries with it any reward."

Later Washington argued that we needed progressivity to obtain necessary revenue: as Eisenhower said at one point, "I need the money." World War II and its extensions, the Korean War, Vietnam, and the cold war, generally meant that the nation needed resources available at any instant in case of war. In the 1950s the nation had a military policy of "massive retaliation," which meant that at one provocation from Moscow we might launch into full-scale war. Progressivity paid for a strong defense budget. In the 1960s and 1970s, progressivity was there to give government funds to build the Great Society. In the 1980s and 1990s progressive taxes were said to be necessary to keep the deficit in check.

Today those arguments have faded. We have even rejected much of the Great Society. Yet progressivity is still here—and doing even more damage, perhaps, than it has at other times. Here's why: we live in a watershed moment. The computer revolution has given enormous wealth to a small group of people—people whom the class-warfare sorts like to target. Even those who have never worried about such things before are now worried about a new, two-class society—the haves, who enjoy the technology bounty and the bounty of the stock markets, versus the have-nots, the children of working people who never got Intel stock options or even bought a mutual fund. Starting new offices and new businesses, and buying home computers are things these people ought to be allowed to do. Progressivity is often what stops them.

Washington is still hard at work maintaining Bastiat's fatal illusion, insisting it can build a better progressivity mousetrap by promising that next time it will devise a progressive system that spares "us" and punishes only "them"—the distant rich. It tells us it will change its definition of *rich* so that those earning under $100,000—or whatever arbitrary figure lawmakers choose to define as rich—get the benefits and those who can "afford" to pay them, those who earn over $100,000, do not. But wherever lawmakers draw their lines, however desperately they try to build a better mousetrap, they cannot keep up with circumstance. The wrong people always end up paying. That, if anything, has been the lesson of progressivity, a lesson we cannot avoid.

Nor, it should be said, could George Harrison. A few years after "Taxman" made its way into the pantheon of rock music, he, Bob Dylan, and Eric Clapton came to the aid of a starving population and put on the Concert for Bangladesh at Madison Square Garden. The event was a smash, marking, as did Paul Simon's later Graceland concerts, the power popular culture has to stir international opinion. The IRS didn't see it that way, though. Harrison was not your typical fat cat: sometimes he forgot to consult his lawyers, or got poor advice. This time he had apparently failed to fill out all the proper paperwork for the charity event, and the greedy hand pursued him for the next eleven years.

10

YOUR RETIREMENT

IN THE SUMMER OF 1998 A MAGAZINE CALLED *WHERE TO Retire* published a feature on desirable places for seniors to spend their sunset years. The top of the list, at least in one respect, was not Naples, Florida, or Phoenix, Arizona. It was Juneau, Alaska. To be sure, the magazine allowed, Juneau had considerable disadvantages. The cost of living was high; summers were short. The only way to get there from the rest of the state was by ferry, boat, or plane and it was far from loved ones. Juneau did boast the beauty of the Mendenhall Glacier, looming at the edge of town.

But that was not why Juneau was on *Where to Retire*'s list. It was there because it had a powerful advantage: for a retired couple with an income around $65,000 and a $250,000 house, the annual tax bill was only $1,701, compared with a national average of $7,626. For more modest couples, tax bills dipped into the low hundreds; for those who hailed from the state, the savings were even greater.

Pets of the Greedy Hand

There's no record yet of retirees flocking like lemmings to Juneau. In reality, northern rainforest is not most Americans' retirement goal. Yet the Juneau model exists as a sort of emblem of the less extreme perversions that face us when we enter what might be called the senior tax trap.

On the surface, the allegations that senior citizens are in a tax trap might seem odd. Seniors are, after all, supposed to be the beneficiaries of everyone else's tax imprisonment. Younger Americans are the ones who pay in. Seniors are the ones who get the payout. They've done their share, and now it is time for them to collect.

It is true that seniors are in many senses the beloved pets of the greedy hand. They receive the majority of American entitlements. The government spends more on their Medicare, their free health service, and Social Security, their public pension, than it spends on defense, servicing the nation's debt, transportation, and unemployment compensation combined. Then there are the numerous freebies and perks available to the over-fifty-five crowd. "Get free prescription drugs," announces an ad in *Where to Retire* under the headline "Look What Seniors Can Get for Free." It then lists two columns of additional gifts: "up to $800 for food," "free legal help," "$7 off your phone bill every month." Then there are all the more familiar little advantages seniors enjoy, from free flu shots to senior discounts.

Younger people sometimes resent this, in something of the same way the losers in despotic lands resented the privileged *nomenklatura*. The feeling comes in spite of themselves. They know they ought to be generous. But they also know that many of the seniors' class advantages come thanks to the seniors' Godzilla of a lobby, the American Association of Retired Persons. Indeed, one reason younger people don't feel that they have to show the kind of support for their parents that the younger generation used to show is that government, through Social Security, Medicare, and a host of other senior bennies, seems to have taken on that job. In an odd way the whole arrangement cuts at the family-support network, pitting the generation of haves against the generations of have-nots. Younger citizens sometimes refer bitterly to the AARP as the AARPN—the "American Association of Retired Persons *Now*."

The Other Side of the Iron Curtain

Yet senior citizens pay a price for their special status. A senior citizen is, after all, an American, and Americans like to consider themselves free agents in a frontier society. When people turn fifty-five, though, they enter a new and socialized world, a world that in some ways is more like the Hungary or Poland of the 1980s than America in the 1990s.

Consider the deal put before us when we finally win the coveted senior label. Taxes and Social Security rules befuddle seniors and prevent them from working when they would like. The limits that these rules put on their money change their private lives, sometimes even determining whether they marry or where they settle—the Juneau option. Medicare and Medicaid curtail their health care choices and even force them to impoverish themselves.

The trouble starts with the senior work bind. One part

of our system—the private-pension part—encourages people to continue working and defer collecting money. Citizens are allowed to tap into their 401(k)'s without penalty from the time they are fifty-five—an age when many "seniors" have new jobs, young marriages, and even—the men among them—young children. Money inside a 401(k) can grow untaxed until a senior citizen reaches seventy. That means it is in a senior citizen's interest to leave that money untouched as long as possible. When that money is withdrawn, particularly in large amounts, it is taxed at very high rates indeed. Long ago our lawmakers decided that 401(k) money—capital gains to every sane person's mind—shouldn't be taxed as capital gains. Instead 401(k) money is taxed as ordinary income, which means it is subject to much higher rates than capital gains. So Americans tend to postpone their collection date, letting the money grow as much as possible.

Idled

But another set of government rules jerks seniors in a different direction. Americans can begin claiming Social Security benefits at age sixty-two. But their benefits are reduced—permanently—if they choose that option. Waiting until age sixty-five is a good idea. And for each year one waits beyond sixty-five, Social Security benefits increase 3 percent. This arrangement seems to be in everyone's interest. It keeps workers working and saves the government money, since one year working is one less year on the government pension.

But what about those who, after thirty or even forty years of working, need their Social Security benefits? If they are in their sixties, they enter what might be called the doldrums of the seventh decade. That is because people who claim those benefits get them with a terrible penalty. Uncle Sam has determined that Social Security beneficiaries mustn't work "too much." In 1996, for example, "too much" was $11,520 a year. If they start a little business or develop any project that earns over that amount—wham, they lose benefits. For every $2 over the limit sixty-two- to sixty-five-year-olds earn through their industry, they lose $1 in benefits. For every $3 that people ages sixty-five to sixty-nine earn over the exemption, they must forego $1. The age limits are set to be increased. If you were born in 1960 or later, your official Social Security retirement age is sixty-seven.

The Social Security Administration doesn't admire seniors' shows of energy, their contributions to the economy, the fact that their little businesses or their employment might generate jobs in their community. To the Administration, money earned this way is simply "excess earnings" and must be punished.

Like all tax rules, this one has its exemptions. In the year of retirement, it is all right for earnings to exceed the annual exempt amount, as long as wages don't exceed a monthly limit. But the self-employed don't get to enjoy the retirement-year exemption. So taking in some clerical work or repairing computers—the very sorts of things that seem well suited to retirees—is out for Mom and Dad even if they are languishing in the greenhouse.

The system's defenders like to point out that the earnings-limit problem does go away when seniors hit seventy. But seventy- or seventy-five-year-olds don't have as much energy as sixty-four-year-olds. The very moment seniors might

establish a new second career after retirement—their sixties—is the very moment they must call a halt to their work.

On top of this comes a tax insult. Social Security is supposed to be *our money*—we paid it into the system, after all,
for all those years, and Uncle Sam calls it a pension. But the
tax man is never far away. It used to be that up to 50 percent
of benefits were subject to tax over a base amount. Recently
lawmakers changed that. Now a full 85 percent of Social
Security benefits are subject to tax. Florida's fast-food
chains would dearly love to employ more seniors, since they
seem to work better and more reliably than teens when it
comes to blending shakes. But blending shakes or working
a few hours a week at the local Wal-Mart, as many hard-
ware junkies would find appealing, would mean they were
earning "too much" and subject them to additional taxes on
Social Security.

Government has other ways of hobbling active people.
Our disability benefits are so generous that they encourage
workers to retire, withdraw, and otherwise stop working in
the economy. The law gives Medicare and Social Security
money to anyone who has worked a certain length of time
and now is disabled or can convince the authorities he is.
Then there is a program called Supplemental Security Income, which gives seniors extra money if they are determined to be in financial need. Given the choice between a
simple job and SSI, many seniors opt for the latter.

And these conundrums are not like the earnings rule.
They don't magically disappear at seventy. The overall effect is to send a clear message: "Don't work." Most particularly, don't start a business or do anything that falls into the
class of self-employment. Government might appear to be
helping senior citizens traverse a bumpy crossing. But such

"help" pushes them to the dole and encourages them to stay there, however unhappy that makes them.

This is something we, in our rights-conscious age, ought to consider. Employers are often blamed for throwing seniors out of jobs. Indeed, Washington's equal-employment lawyers help citizens who feel they have faced age discrimination to sue employers. But the worst offender, the biggest age discriminator, is not the private sector. It is the senior tax trap, which idles tens of thousands every year.

The Big Tax Punishment

When seniors do start to collect their 401(k) money, another blow comes. In the olden days, capital gains were capital gains and were taxed as such. This is no longer so. If a capital gain is inside a 401(k) or any other tax-protected mechanism, it grows there unchecked. But when citizens draw down their money, it is taxed at our nation's highest statutory rates for living people. Instead of paying low capital-gains rates on their money, seniors can pay top marginal rates of up to 39.6 percent.

All these factors combine to do something very un-American. They lock seniors into a permanent mind-set of dependency, a mind-set they themselves may not have chosen. They are forced into what might be called the fixed-income club. They can only earn so much, so their fixed income is the only pie they have.

Life in the fixed-income club is unnerving. Psychologists tell us that the best thing for seniors is to make them feel independent and strong. Most seniors strive to be independent. Living on a fixed income puts them in the opposite situation. It means being vulnerable to whatever winds the economy or government stirs up. In the 1970s, for example, inflation impoverished many thousands by rendering their entitlements far too deficient to cover their costs. When home prices rise or rent control ends, the fixed-income crowd is the set that loses. When taxes climb—as they have in places like New York, Chicago, and San Francisco—the fixed-income crowd can't afford the change.

The fixed-income problem goes a long way toward explaining why what seem paltry tax advantages to working people are enough to pull seniors to Juneau—or Midland, Texas, or Naples, Florida, to name other low-tax destinations. It explains why they are so often penny-pinchers, why they fuss in movie lines about senior discounts, and why they attend the bargain matinee on Tuesday. They need every nickel.

Seniors try to move lightly in their chains. They say they like to go to matinees on Tuesday. They point out that there are many reasons they are happy to move to Florida. They tout the advantages of the weather and the breezes. They call themselves "snowbirds." But some snowbirds feel caged. They are idle—and bored—in Florida and Palm Springs. Not everyone wants to miss the sight of their grandchild's first step or their first piano recital. But often they have to, because staying near their children costs too much.

Infantilized

The fixed-income problem also reveals why many seniors lobby so tenaciously against all change, be it the lifting of rent control, the end of bus subsidies, or sensible tax reform.

Trapped in the golden prison of senior welfare, they have little choice but to act like citizens on the dole and fight every change. This is at best counterproductive and at worst terribly demoralizing. To protect our parents, the system infantilizes them.

Medicare is one of the big infantilizers. The rest of us longingly eye the program: who wouldn't want guaranteed health care for something close to free? Well, it turns out that many seniors don't. That's because Medicare severely curtails the way they handle their illnesses. It does pay for them to have endless CAT scans and expensive procedures. But it doesn't pay for the thing most seniors need, the thing that keeps them out of the hospital: prescription drugs.

Medicare has other horrors. Because it is a price-control system, it converts seniors into second-class health care customers. Urologists and gynecologists get less money for checking a prostate or doing a Pap smear for a senior than they would for providing precisely the same service to younger people. Up to 30 percent less, a serious amount in these days of health care as business. So doctors often don't like to take these patients. It is no wonder seniors spend so much time in mechanized phone queues waiting to get an appointment.

Drive-through Mastectomies

There are more dramatic examples. In 1997 the newspapers and members of Congress began talking about a new example of modern medical cost-cutting: the drive-through mastectomy. Hospitals and doctors were telling women to return home from the hospital the same day they underwent this deeply traumatic operation. Many doctors said women actually preferred this. But most people were horrified at the thought that patients had no choice in the matter.

Much of the coverage of the drive-through mastectomy blamed the frightful story on managed care. Cruel HMO's, the reporting went, were to blame for the change. But when *The Wall Street Journal*'s editors looked at the data, we found an astounding thing. The highest incidences of drive-through mastectomies weren't occurring in managed-care patients. They were occurring in Medicare patients. And no wonder: government was pushing seniors' doctors and hospitals to reduce patient hospital stays any way they could.

Even when a senior has enough money to do what any other American would do in the same situation—opt out of the socialist construct and pay a little more for better service—the system makes sure he can't do that. For many years Medicare regulators have pressured doctors into refusing citizens this choice. In 1997 our government took the craziness one step further. It slapped an enormous punishment on doctors who dared to work in the free market: if they contracted with even a single senior patient to provide services outside the Medicare system, they couldn't take any Medicare patients for the following two years. The effect was to padlock seniors into Medicare's program.

Younger people also suffer from the Medicare machine. Hospitals and doctors don't eat the costs they incur when Medicare underpays them. They merely shift those costs to the rest of the country. Working families carry the load of seniors' unpaid bills in the form of higher health-insurance premiums. Indeed, cost shifting pushes health-insurance prices for average citizens into the stratosphere, which is one reason tens of millions of American children don't get the basic coverage our society gives their grandparents.

Granny Goes to Jail

There is a final Medicare perversity. The moment seniors really need health care—the moment they fall victim to a serious, long-term illness—Medicare shuts down. Seniors who must be in hospitals or assisted-care homes for a year or more can get Medicaid. But since the rules say that Medicaid is a program for the poor, they have to impoverish themselves to be eligible. This is good for lawyers, who do a fine business rearranging senior citizens' assets so that they look poor. But it's rotten for seniors, who sometimes must part from their families to meet the exacting requirements of Medicaid. They know there is something unethical and destructive in parting with their financial independence in this manner. Yet holding on to their money turns them into criminals: Medicaid-fraud prosecution was so vigorous in the mid-1990s that it came to be known as the "Granny goes to jail" problem. Congress had to work to insert a provision in tax law to stop lawyers from persecuting eighty-five-year-old ladies with broken hips.

"Too Many Workers"

Like all tax traps, the senior tax traps come out of a time in the nation's history when we viewed things differently. Social Security, for example, dates back to when nobody expected people to live much beyond the age of sixty-five, let alone want to work. Today people routinely live ten or fifteen

years beyond that, but Social Security's budget still operates as if it were a one- or five-year arrangement.

Social Security's earnings rule, the rule that locks people
in their sixties into work purgatory, is the direct result of
New Deal thinking. Economists in those days, as well as officials in FDR's brain trust, thought that the cause of the
Depression was "too much labor." The legislators who
wrote the Social Security law focused on this, seeing the
Social Security program as a useful buyout that would save
jobs for younger workers who "needed" them. So they in-
tentionally idled seniors.

Today most economists will tell you that those
Depression-era thinkers were wrong. In reality the Depression had other sources—bad policy at the Federal Reserve,
tax increases, tariffs, global collapse, an overall lack of confidence. And today we have record-low unemployment.
Firms are actually begging for workers. Yet the system is
still busy forcing seniors out to pasture as if they represented some kind of major economic threat.

Living in Sin

Then there is the senior marriage penalty, the corollary
to the one younger couples face. Our graduated tax system was designed to punish the rich. No one in our society
wants to see seniors spend their last years alone. Yet when
two senior citizens of moderate income marry, they often
find themselves facing the marriage penalty. Suddenly they
are in a higher tax bracket and are taxed as though
they were rich. They also often begin to lose Social Security
benefits or, for example, Medicaid. No wonder that many

oldsters often choose to "live in sin." Explaining to children about "Grandma's friend" or "Uncle Joe" has become a routine part of the family drive down to visit grandparents in Florida.

The Medicare plan comes straight out of Lyndon Johnson's Great Society and a vision of Big Government as efficient and necessary. The bitter lesson of Medicare, though, has been that Big Government, even in a capitalist context, doesn't work. Today everyone realizes this: President Clinton's ill-fated health care reform was an effort, however maladroit, to reintroduce the market into the health care process. Republicans have tried to reintroduce choice through medical savings accounts. Yet Medicare is a hard program to cut: seniors, stuck in their fixed-income traps, are understandably reluctant to trade it for an unknown quantity. When Republicans tried to restrain Medicare growth in the mid-1990s, Democrats ran scare ads to frighten seniors. It worked, and the senior citizens voted Democratic.

Baby Boomers Come Next

Working our way out of the senior tax trap will prove one of our greatest challenges: nothing is harder to undo than a massive entitlement whose beneficiaries include the middle class. And the AARP has done a brilliant job lobbying for benefits over the years. It hasn't done much, though, to win seniors what they most need in these days: freedom and flexibility. Sixty Plus, another senior lobby, is fighting for privatization of Social Security, so that future seniors will enjoy better returns than the limited sums available to current oldsters. But generally politicians, Republican and

Democrat alike, tend to mistake the senior lobbies for seniors themselves. This even though seniors themselves have repeatedly shown enthusiasm for reforms, including privatization of Social Security.

Yet there is an urgency to change. In coming years the Depression crowd will not be the ones in the senior club. It will be the baby boomers' turn. Baby boomers have spent years proving their self-reliance. Unless they take up the topic, they will be the next ones inside the senior cage.

11

YOUR DEATH

IN DECEMBER 1988, LIFE TURNED BLACK FOR A NEW YORK couple named John and Barbara Zwynenburg. They learned that their twenty-nine-year-old son Mark, an investment banker with Goldman Sachs, had gone down with Pan Am's Flight 103 from London to New York. The couple and Mark's surviving brother were told his remains were somewhere in the debris around Lockerbie, Scotland. For the family, a long period of mourning began. They hoped for a settlement from Pan Am. They tried to work with the State Department to bring the terrorists to justice.

But it was not diplomats or government-information officers who responded first to the Zwynenburgs' grief. It was the IRS. One day the family received one of the Service's famous deficiency notices—a report that said they owed back taxes. Not just a small amount either: $6 million on the settlement the IRS estimated they would receive from Pan Am's insurers. The IRS was demanding the money now—even before the Zwynenburgs received their settlement. At first, the Zwynenburgs told the papers, they thought the letter was a joke. When they realized it wasn't, they began to reel.

John Zwyenburg tried to articulate the family's incomprehension in an interview with CNN's Donna Kelley. He wondered aloud why the U.S. government was concentrating on harassing families for revenue rather than chasing the Libyan terrorists. "This is small potatoes, this is trash," he commented on the IRS problem. "The issue is really terrorism, the bombing of Pan Am 103." He summed up: "That's where they should be focusing, so they don't continue to attack the American people." The most galling aspect of the episode is that the IRS didn't consider it exceptional. As the agency's lawyers saw it, the IRS was pursuing revenue that rightly belonged to it. The Zwynenburgs had to pay thousands in attorneys' fees to fend off the government in its pursuit of money the family wasn't even sure of ever seeing. Barbara Zwynenburg reports, years later, that the IRS's guesstimate of their settlement was grossly inflated; their final compensation for their loss ran in the thousands, not the millions.

The dunning of the Zwynenburgs was just one of thousands of unnecessary American misfortunes, smaller and bigger, that happen each year because of what are known as estate taxes. The estate tax and its sibling, the gift tax, are unusual creatures in the world of the federal tax code, for several reasons. The first is that they are a wealth tax. A wealth tax is an intrusive thing that seems more appropriate for Europe with its institutionalized class warfare than the United States. It punishes taxpayers just for having money, no matter how they acquired it. If this seems hard to understand, just think of the estate tax as a tax on virtue. Penurious senior citizens save because they want to leave money for their children. Yet the more they save, the more their children lose.

The second thing estate taxes do is undermine families by sundering the physical things that have come to hold meaning for them. Jane Smiley laid this out beautifully in her novel *A Thousand Acres,* a modern retelling of Shakespeare's *King Lear.* Larry Cook, the dark patriarch, doesn't want the government to cut up the farm he has spent his life building. The prospect of estate taxes drives him to divide his property and give it to his daughters before his death. "Anyway, if I died tomorrow, you would have to pay seven or eight hundred thousand dollars' inheritance tax," Cook tells his daughters.

In this tale, as is often the case in real life, other, larger forces pull at the family fabric. But the passing reference to the tax threat gives *A Thousand Acres* a contemporary resonance.

The third thing about estate taxes is that they catch us at a vulnerable moment. The government collects its estate tax from people at the moment they are often least equipped to object: the moment of their death. Opponents of the estate tax call it "the death tax." The title sounds hyperbolic, but in this instance it is justified.

Estate taxes work by stealth. If we die with assets worth less than $600,000—the amount that is, at this writing, exempt from the estate tax—we don't have to worry about this levy. But many of us aren't the sort to plan what our exact net worth will be at the hour of our death. We also, of course, do not know exactly when that moment is coming. And if, at the crucial hour, we are worth something over that amount, even just a penny over, we are trapped. The rate starts at 18 percent and climbs from there to 55 percent or above. Our heirs confront a reduced inheritance.

The federal estate tax isn't the whole story. States have

their estate taxes too, often wicked ones. New York has some of the worst, which is one reason, as its governor said, "it's not just the weather that makes people move to Florida or Arizona."

Tax writers often claim they are doing us a favor when they pass an estate tax. They rush to point out that in the next decade the law will change, so that only estates of over $1 million will face the tax. They insist, too, that they have crafted the tax into a mild-mannered, unintrusive little thing. They point out that the estate tax isn't a problem for widows or widowers. There is no estate tax when a spouse dies and leaves his or her worldly goods to the surviving partner. The estate tax only comes into play when money is passing from one generation to the next.

Strange as it may sound, the theory here is that death is the least painful moment for the greedy hand to do its work. The tax writers wax poetic, describing the moment after death as an ephemeral interlude, the interregnum when the money and property involved belong to "no one"—neither to the dead person nor yet to his heirs. At that moment, the government says, "this money is no one's, so it is mine."

Needless to say, people who end up paying the levy don't share this view. The moment that a family member dies is an intensely private moment. It is the moment people most want their family, and the family jewels in the crypt, to be left alone. To them the government seems like an ambulance chaser, even a grave robber. The fact that their small—or not-so-small—consolation for the death, their inheritance, is unexpectedly being tampered with tends to provoke outright rage.

Some of the bigger estate tax targets are family enterprises—a farm, a Burger King franchise, a lumber business. That's because these businesses, while valuable—many are worth more than the "rich guy" million dollar cut-off— don't always throw off much cash. To pay the estate-tax bill, families must often break up the family treasure. It's a bitter thing: along with the founder, families lose what the founder built.

One of the best examples of the estate tax's range and de- struction is the case of sports moguls, the O'Malley family. The O'Malleys are a clan so mighty they can break a city's heart. They broke Brooklyn's in 1957, when they removed the Dodgers from their home and transplanted them to Los Angeles. In 1997 it was Los Angelinos' turn for heartbreak. Pete O'Malley, the head of the family business, announced he was putting the Dodgers up for sale. But the real heart- break this time was the O'Malleys'. Because of the estate tax, Pete O'Malley couldn't do what he might otherwise have done: leave his team to his thirteen heirs. The estate tax forced him to give up ownership of his family team and offer it to strangers without ties to L.A. The Dodgers went to Fox, Rupert Murdoch's North American conglomerate. L.A. citizens are well aware that team owners are moody and fickle. Now they fear that Mr. Murdoch will take the Dodgers away.

Another estate-tax target was a fourth-grader who won *National Geographic*'s geography bee for his school, beating seventh- and eighth-graders. His mother, Jeannine Mizell, would dearly like to save her money to put him through a good college. That too was what the child's grandfather had wanted: he squirreled away certificates of deposit, bank ac- counts, and stocks. When that grandfather died, though, his family paid a terrible estate-tax penalty. The tax claimed $150,000 from the lean family business, Mizell Lumber. The causes of the charge were accidents of history: the father had purchased the firm's land for $55,000 many years ago, and now that land had appreciated. Unlike the pluto-crats' paintings, that land was taxable at its appreciated value. "To our surprise and chagrin," Jeannine Mizell re-called when she testified on the story before Congress, "we owed a whopping $297,000 in federal taxes." It took the family $40,000 in attorney and appraisal fees, as well as two and a half years of distraction, to settle the Mizell Lumber estate.

Many small businesses do escape the estate tax—but at what seems a prohibitive price. Cold Spring Construction, an Akron, New York, firm threatened by the estate tax, had done a lot for its community. Cold Spring employed mem-bers of the Forrestel family, the owners, giving jobs to twenty children, nieces, and nephews every summer they were in college. It supported 150 families from the Akron area, a depressed region where employment has often been hard to find. Yet in recent years the company had had to turn its resources from growth or job creation. Instead of in-vesting in equipment, manpower, and technology, Richard Forrestel, Jr., told congressional aides, the firm had to invest in arming itself to handle the estate tax. It spent over $2 mil-lion on insurance and accounting just so it would have the money when the time came to pay its bills. Nor is Cold Spring alone: a full 62 percent of members of the Associated General Contractors of America buy mostly unnecessary life-insurance policies in order to ward off the same foe.

Indeed, economists believe that the estate tax, that

ephemeral levy, is a major killer of family businesses. Only 30 percent of family businesses make it to the next generation; that figure drops to 13 percent for the third generation. A study by the American Family Business Institute found that the principal cause of the death of these businesses, second only to the damage done when a founder dies, was the estate tax.

This pain is gratuitous because the estate tax is not even an efficient tax. Economists recently ran the numbers and found that for the $19 billion in federal death taxes collected last year, taxpayers spent $25 billion in time and energy avoiding them. They spend that money out of fear that they *might* be subject to the tax. Indeed, experts who looked into the matter for Congress found that in a recent year, 1995, 70,000 families went through the trouble of filing estate-tax returns, but only 31,000 of those estates ended up actually being subject to tax.

Precisely how we got to this point is worth mulling over, if only because the estate tax is the last, best example, a gem of an example, of how even the tiniest of plans to tax "the rich" backfire, raining trouble on all the rest of us. The story starts with our founders, who wanted America to be a land of opportunity. The image of Europe, a continent divided into a rigid class system of winners—the gentry—and losers—the common man—haunted them. In their time Europe, and the new America, were still largely agricultural. But for the exception of a slender stratum of tradesmen, there were two classes of people: those who had land and those who didn't.

Those who had land were the titled rich. Those who didn't were indentured servants, tenant farmers, or slaves.

Inheriting land meant inheriting wealth. This held true even for kings: long after we recall why, we retain the names of the royals who didn't have land, and what they did to obtain it: John Lackland, his very name marking his humiliating status, waging war to change that status.

Our national fathers sought to right things in young America. They tried to make land ownership a little more egalitarian. They fought primogeniture, and from time to time they supported certain wealth taxes. Indeed, Tom Paine, a product of King George's England, actually *liked* the idea of deploying the greedy hand. His social security plan was based on an inheritance tax. The young nation tried an estate tax—to build the navy, in 1797. But citizens of young America used force to convince their government that they thought estate taxes, along with other taxes, were a bad idea. The estate tax disappeared along with the excise on whiskey and other hated internal taxes.

In this century progressives led the way in establishing the estate tax. Again, their goal was to level the rich. Theodore Roosevelt said it was time to stop "the transmission in their entirety of those fortunes swollen beyond all healthy limits." But it was Teddy Roosevelt's cousin, Franklin, who put through the heaviest of estate taxes. One of the most picturesque of the loopholes that came out of this was the so-called "flower bonds." As the writer John Steele Gordon details in his remarkable book on the national debt, *Hamilton's Blessings,* flower bonds were long-term Treasuries that paid very low interest, so that they traded far below face value. But the federal government would accept them as tender at their face value. So people rushed to use them to pay their estate taxes. As Gordon notes, nobody in good health wanted to hold these bad bonds. And they could not be bought after a death to pay the bills of the estate. So people tended to buy them at the very last minute, shortly before it came time to select the flowers for the funeral. The "flower bonds" appellation makes the securities seem quaint. But many decades later, one still has to ask: did the families need the extra aggravation?

In reality, inheritance and death taxes have always been at odds with American society. That's because a permanent, landed aristocracy has never reigned in America, at least not for any protracted period. *Wealth* reigns—in Southampton, Long Island, or on San Francisco's Russian Hill. But the families who are wealthy are not always the same families, at least not for long. Bill and Melinda Gates, one of America's richest couples, come straight from America's middle class. Americans move up and down the economic scale with incredible speed: the data show that downward mobility is as big a part of our economic culture as our storied ascents. As long ago as the 1840s, this was clear to observers. Tocqueville wondered at the American way in his *Democracy in America:* "The aspect of American society is animated because men and things are always changing."

Today, more than ever, the intent of the estate-tax writers is not realized. The estate tax fails entirely to punish the rich the way they planned. In fact, the estate-tax scenario is one in which the rich and the near-rich almost always win. IRS data show that it captured income from only 245 estates worth over $20 million in a recent year.

Monied Americans have turned estate-tax avoidance into

an intricate art. They start by assembling their children for long meetings in law offices, accounting offices, offices of real estate appraisers. They delve into acronyms. They fiddle with Q-TIPs (qualified terminable-interest property trusts). They learn about CRATs and CLATs, CLUTs and CRUTs (if one really must know, these letters stand for charitable remainder annuity trusts, charitable lead annuity trusts, charitable lead unitrusts, and charitable remainder unitrusts, respectively). They sign a paradoxical-sounding document called a "living will." They ponder private foundations. They give their property to museums and get annuities, which keep them in comfort and transfer their estates to their children or grandchildren more or less intact.

The estate tax is particularly kind to people who have been lucky already and inherited valuable things long ago. It treads gently around plutocrat art collectors. Many of them, or their parents, bought paintings and sculptures in the 1940s and early 1950s, when Monets, Vuillards, and that Brancusi on the lawn were begging for buyers in shabby postwar Europe. Today many of the well-to-do inheritors of art are clever enough to plop title to their treasures in the safe haven of a CRAT. If they fashion the arrangement right, they can even sell these treasures without any tax, reinvest the money, and live off it before they die.

Town & Country magazine laid out this entire story in a 1995 encomium to estate planning it wrote on Jacqueline Kennedy Onassis. With the aid of her beau, Maurice Tempelsman, and, doubtless, uncounted lawyers, Mrs. Onassis managed to turn her estate, worth well over $100 million, into something her dear ones could use. She left her children

$250,000 each, as well as her homes in Martha's Vineyard and on New York's Upper East Side. She gave Mr. Tempelsman a Greek alabaster head of a woman, a souvenir of their time together. And she optimized the CLAT loophole by creating a foundation, the C & J Foundation, for Caroline and John. The CLAT rules required that the foundation make charitable gifts worth 8 percent of its original value every year for twenty-four years. This ensured—as if it needed ensuring—that John and Caroline would remain popular dinner guests in New York for that period. At the end of the twenty-four years the money is to go back to the Kennedys. But not Jackie's children: to avoid tax penalties it skips generations and goes to the grandchildren. The cleverness of this labyrinthine arrangement—all perfectly legal—was Topic A among the Park Avenue set for several months after Mrs. Onassis's untimely death.

But most people can't afford a string of attorneys, and some of them do end up paying taxes that surround death. In the Kennedy story there was even such a figure, although strictly speaking it was income tax, not estate tax, that punished her. The woman, named Susan Krupski Fisher, happened to buy a $20 box of chocolates at Godiva, the chocolatier. Inside the box—one she bought at the Love Lane Sweet Shop in Mattituck, Long Island—was news of a stupendous prize. As part of a Valentine's Day promotion, Godiva was giving one lucky buyer a famous ruby, emerald, and diamond necklace that had once belonged to Jackie O.

The tax bill on the $156,000 necklace, though, was $45,000—far too much for the medical secretary and her husband. "We're ordinary people," Krupski Fisher told the *New York Post,* which carried the story. "It's way out of my league." Krupski Fisher posed in the string of Burma rubies and rondels of diamonds for the paper's cameras. Then she sold the necklace, and paid her taxes.

Most Americans are more like Susan Krupski Fisher than like Jackie O. We find the estate tax is a penalty that cuts into our private lives. Congress recently passed laws to raise the amount exempt from the estate tax to over a million dollars. But even that high-sounding limit will hit some very average-seeming family businesses.

And this "tax on the rich" does particularly dirty work on a group our society wants to move forward: minorities. Sylvia's, a Harlem soul-food restaurant, is a good example. The restaurant was founded by Sylvia herself, as a small place. But today it is one of Harlem's success stories. It has grown to be a hot tourist destination and also sells a line of soul-food sauces. The manager is Sylvia's son, Van Woods.

Woods used to be something of a social revolutionary. He worked with the government to get social services to help poor people. He even named his son Che, after Che Guevara, the Communist guerrilla. But today Woods is an amateur lobbyist against the estate tax. That's because handing Sylvia's down to younger generations will trigger taxes so heavy they will have to break up the restaurant and everything the family has built.

Such pinches have outsized economic costs. It's hard to quantify precisely the benefit the nation could see from repealing the estate tax. But one set of numbers, derived through a model from an economic consultancy called the WEFA Group, found that the gains would be significant. The numbers showed that the economy would grow by $11 billion every year if there were no estate tax. It would create 145,000 jobs, not a huge number but enough to make a labor secretary, or a handful of congressmen, feel good for an afternoon.

Nonetheless, there's a sort of crude justice to the fact that this ghoulish, antiquated levy has survived and thrived even into our own era. Live by taxes, die by them, the estate tax tells us. The greedy hand wouldn't live up to its name if it didn't make this last grab.

Conclusion: Your Choice

Americans today are more prosperous than we have ever been. As a nation, we have come very far, so far that even our past is beginning to look different. In the 1960s, 1970s, and even the 1980s, we took Big Government America, the America of the postwar period, to be the only America, an America that permanently supplanted something antiquated. This conviction strengthened when we considered the enormous troubles that plagued us in those decades. Who else but government could end the underclass, right the wrongs of Vietnam, combat inflation?

We can see now that in those years we had a foreshortened view of history. From the heights of our new achievement, we recognize that the Great Society, for all its ideals, was something of an aberration. It is clear now that the self-doubt and gray misgivings of the Vietnam period were, in their way, just a momentary interruption. The inflation of the 1970s was an acute and terrible problem but a short-lived one. Our famous deficit agony—which so many commentators and foreigners alleged would bring us down—has, at least for the moment, receded. Today we are in many ways more like the America of

Andrew Jackson or even Thomas Jefferson than we are like the America of Jimmy Carter.

This change was the result of enormous and serious work. We developed microchips and computers that secured our global economic dominance. We started the welfare state and then, when we saw it wasn't working, successfully ended it. We grew a stock market that will provide pensions for the baby boom and beyond. Serious challenges loom ahead. Unpredictable rogue states threaten our national security; the economy will not always live up to its 1990s boom. But we understand now that the key to sustaining our prosperity is recognizing that we are our own best providers. Thinkers from left, center, and right agree: we don't need a nanny state.

This American confidence is not new. It is simply a homecoming to older ideals, ideals that we held through most of our history. Self-reliance is the ultimate American tradition. Even through a good part of the Depression "no handouts" was Americans' self-imposed rule. We are coming to a new appreciation of what Tocqueville admiringly called "self-interest, rightly understood."

Yet we are still saddled with our tax structure, the unwieldy artifact of an irrelevant era.

Unburdening ourselves is not easy, but it is something we have in our power to do. Our impasse, in fact, contains the outline of its own solution, if only we allow ourselves to look at it clearly. What, exactly, does our long struggle with Paine's greedy hand tell us?

Taxes have to be visible. Beardsley Ruml's trap worked because it made taxes invisible. No one today willingly gives a third or a half of his income into a strange hand; we only pay our taxes now because the trap locked shut long ago. We never see our tax bill in its entirety except during the madness of filing season.

When we rewrite our arrangement with government, we need to write into it a tax structure that is clear and comprehensible, whose outlines we can see and consider whenever we choose.

Taxes have to be simple. The tax code is a monster of complexity, but it doesn't have to be. When rules are added to rules, the change may benefit certain classes, but they hurt the rest of us. The best thing is to settle on one system, even if someone shouts that it's not "fair" to everyone.

Taxes are for revenue. For fifty years we have used taxes to steer behavior. Indeed, politicians often used the argument that they were promoting social good through the tax code as window dressing for their real aim: getting at the revenue. None of us likes the result. We are responsible for our own fate; let government take what we choose to give it and then retreat.

Taxes have to be lower. We have managed to achieve prosperity notwithstanding high taxes. But that prosperity would have been greater without those taxes. The microchip, in its way, has allowed us to postpone our date with tax reform.

But epochal transformations like the computer revolution, or the Industrial Revolution for that matter, cannot be counted on to come every decade. Taxes will slow our economy if we don't bring them down to rates that allow us to sustain desirable growth.

We don't have to load extra taxes on the rich. We've learned that a tax system that punishes the rich also punishes the rest of us. Those who have money should pay taxes like everyone else. In fact the rich already carry more of the tax burden than any other income group. Yet history—the history of the 1980s in particular—has shown an amazing thing—that lower rates on the rich produce more revenue from them.

Progressivity has had its day. Let us move on to a tax system that is more worthy of us, one that makes sense for the country.

It's time to privatize Social Security. Many of the core tax problems we face today are in reality Social Security problems. Markets have taught us that they can do a better job than government in providing public pensions. We should privatize a portion of Social Security—at least three of the percentage points that individuals carry.

The only thing to guard against is a privatization that is not a true privatization. When government enters the stock market on behalf of citizens, as many advocates of Social Security privatization would like, that is not privatization. That is expanding the public sector at the cost of the private sector. An office in government that invests on behalf of citizens, as many are proposing, is an office open to enormous moral hazard. To understand this you need only to consider what would happen if the chairman of the Securities and Exchange Commission directly controlled a few hundred million shares of blue-chip stocks.

Individuals need to control their own accounts, just as they control the rest of their money. Government guarantees of returns are also guarantees of disaster. One need only look to our recent history with savings and loans to see that. Raising the ceiling on federal insurance of S & L accounts led to that disaster by giving S & L directors license without accountability. The cost ran into the hundreds of billions, but it was far lower than the cost a government guarantee on privatized Social Security would be.

Local is good. The enduring lesson of our schools crisis is that centralizing school finance to the state and federal level has not given us the equity or the academic performance we hoped for. These results have ramifications far beyond schools. The federal government cannot solve everything. Many problems—from school to health care to welfare—are better handled lower down. A wise tax reform is a tax reform that leaves much of the nation's work to the people and the officials they know. Trying to write a federal tax law that addresses all our national problems is a recipe for a repeat of the current trouble.

We must lock in change. In the 1980s, through tremendous political and social exertion, the nation joined together to lower tax rates and prune out many of the code's absurdities. Within a few years, Washington had destroyed its own child. This time we must fix our change so the fiddlers can't get at it.

Once we know where we are, putting through change is not so hard. We can replace the current system with a national sales tax, the kind advocated by the chairman of the House Ways and Means Committee, Bill Archer. We can do away with the constraining code and have everyone choose when they pay taxes by choosing what they purchase. Chairman Archer has even built into his system a plan to make it fair for poor people. He will give them a tax exemption for the first $20,000 or $30,000 they spend to be sure that their lives are not eaten away by taxes.

But there are problems with a national sales tax. One is this: in nearly every country where it has been tried, whatever the political promises, a sales tax has come *in addition* to an income tax, not instead of one. A sales tax means a tax on services, which means that when we buy homes, when we pay a plumber, we will have to tack on a 15 or 20 percent tax. That's too much. In Europe, where value-added taxes have long reigned, they have done much to sour the political culture.

Heavy sales taxes have helped render Europe a continent of scofflaws, not just when it comes to nanny taxes, but in every regard. America is too good for that.

Then there is the flat tax as proposed by House Majority leader Dick Armey. It would sweep away the code, and it would support lower earners. It would help them with a general tax exemption of up to $34,000 for a household. But it too is a radical measure, particularly when it comes to business taxes. It would involve disruption. That disruption would become more than worth the price if we could assure ourselves that we were locking in the change.

A third and serviceable option is simply to clear out the underbrush and put through lower, simpler rates that apply to all in a consistent matter. Our political leaders can do this if they throw away the distribution tables that have made tax writing a Procrustean bed in the modern era. If the "middle class" appears to come off a little better than the poor, that is not so bad. America, after all, is not feudal France or the czar's Russia. Mobility studies show that in this country, today's poor are tomorrow's middle class. This is the level of reform, by the way, that many Americans support.

Most Americans are not fire-breathing radicals or Ruby Ridge survivalists. They don't want to "kill the IRS." They just want a common-sense change in the system. And that is what they are telling lawmakers. When Steve LaTourette, a Republican congressman from Ohio, surveyed his constituents, he found that just about half wanted the IRS abolished. But a full three quarters wanted to see the tax code itself abolished. They saw that the code, not the bureaucrats, was the problem.

The second part of the program is to make the change truly

permanent through a constitutional amendment. Our nation's last experience of trying to pass a significant-seeming constitutional amendment—the Equal Rights Amendment—was a bitter one. It soured Washington on amendments in general. Hesitation over amendments goes a long way toward explaining the current Republican foundering.

A constitutional amendment that calls for limiting federal taxes, including Social Security, to 25 percent of our income, or even a lower share, would be an important first step out of the logjam. For one thing, states would have to ratify the change, and that would allow us to have a much needed national discussion about taxes. Citizens would have to consider what lawmakers were proposing. This would give voters a chance to get around the lobbies and politicians who have kept the tax debate to themselves. It would get us all back into the discussion.

The third step is to realize that as a people we want to pay taxes. Roosevelt called taxes "the dues we pay for organized society." We still feel that way.

But people want a tax system that doesn't intrude on our private lives while it collects those dues; and we want those dues to be spent in a reasonable, limited way. We want a tax code that, to quote former Treasury secretary William Simon again, looks as if somebody designed it on purpose. Not a giant machine that collects our money merely to feed the monster.

Over the years at *The Wall Street Journal,* the editors have pondered all these solutions. The main challenge that has faced us is how to get around the politics. But this is not impossible.

Take one proposal put forward by Stephen Moore of the Cato Institute, called the alternative maximum tax. The max tax, as it has also been called, would give taxpayers a choice: keep paying under the old system if the math works out better for them. But if it doesn't, take a new system: pay a flat rate of something like 25, 23, or 20 percent.

The ingenious aspect of this is that it defangs the lobbies. If millions of old people choose to take the flat rate, the AARP can no longer argue that a flat tax is "bad for senior citizens." If millions of home owners take the flat rate, then the real estate lobby can no longer complain that America can't do without the home-mortgage deduction. If millions of municipal bond-holders opt for the flat tax, then the municipal-bond lobby's argument for its special exemption becomes fainter. The max tax has the power to muffle Gucci Gulch's roar, to expose the lobbies as secondary and dispensable.

Politicians are not necessarily the enemies here. They too are stuck in the grip of Paine's greedy hand. Indeed, when we all arrive at the right place, then politicians can help us. They are eager to do so. The 1998 revamp of the IRS, which the Senate backed in an unmistakable 96 0 vote, is a measure of their understanding that things have to change with tax. Members of Congress from Dick Gephardt to Dick Armey have plugged for a flatter code. Daniel Patrick Moynihan of New York has railed against complexity. Dennis Hastert, the new Speaker of the House, says Americans "don't want to pass more and more of their paychecks to a tax collector." Senator William Roth, the Finance Committee chairman, is equally committed. The politicians know that if they have our help, they can affect change.

It is important to remember that luck is on our side. Today the nation is actually in a better position to undertake a tax reform than at any point in living memory. In the 1980s, the last time the nation took up tax reform, the lawmakers had a much harder job. With the deficit ballooning to record proportion, they got sidetracked in a pointless budgetary battle. In those years, too, the nation was still committed, mentally and financially, to spend its way toward Lyndon Johnson's Great Society. In the 1960s, when John Kennedy and his Treasury secretary, Douglas Dillon, took up tax reform, they were at the helm of a nation in a state of siege, a nation that needed to marshal every resource to combat Khrushchev and face off with Communist China. Today we have no deficit and no cold war.

We need only to look to our own history for the path to follow. The Continental Congress and the young America raised internal taxes. The result was the Whiskey Rebellion and the violence of Daniel Shays. Thomas Jefferson, a lawmaker of the sort today's politicians might like to model themselves after, heeded the people. He campaigned on tax reform in 1800. In 1805, with his second inaugural address, he summarized his implementation of the people's desires: "The suppression of unnecessary offices, of useless establishments and expenses, enabled us to discontinue our internal taxes. These covering our land with officers, and opening our doors to their intrusions, had already begun that process of domicilary vexation which, once entered, is scarcely to be restrained from reaching successively every article of produce and property."

We too can suppress our unnecessary offices and cut back our tax state. When we do we will truly be Jefferson's people again: a nation where, as he drew the picture, "it may be the pleasure and pride of an American to ask, what farmer, what mechanic, what laborer, ever sees a tax-gatherer of the United States?"

At the turn of the century the author Ben Hecht described the America he saw: "The young century wore a merry, untaxed look. People could get rich without cheating the government." Today people again manage to find prosperity without cheating the government. But imagine what we could find if the next century, too, started its course merry and untaxed.

Indeed, in *Rights of Man,* the book where he first gave us the image of the greedy hand, Thomas Paine also wrote of how that hand might be vanquished. Citizens merely needed the political will to change. "If systems of government can be introduced less expensive and more productive of general happiness than those which have existed," Paine concluded, "all attempts to oppose their progress will in the end be fruitless."

Acknowledgments

THE ERRORS IN THIS BOOK ARE ALL MY OWN. THAT THERE are not more of them is thanks to many people, so many that I can't mention them all. In particular I'd like to single out: Tom Field and Joe Thorndike at the journal *Tax Notes,* who generously opened the door to their world, a world made entirely of taxes. Chris Frenze and Andy Laperriere reviewed the Earned Income Credit and other complexities with me numerous times. Dick Armey and Steve Forbes both talked through various questions. Ways and Means chairman Bill Archer and his noble staffer, Ari Fleischer, worked through the question of tax reform with me. Fred Goldberg, a former IRS commissioner, read parts of the manuscript. The book has benefited from a talk with Michael Graetz, Yale University's tax sage. Rose and Milton Friedman gave inspiring advice. Bruce Bartlett read parts of the manuscript.

Grace-Marie Arnett of the Galen Institute opened my eyes to the tax relevance of Medicare. J. D. Foster and Patrick Fleenor of the Tax Foundation faxed many charts and talked through numerous points. June O'Neill, former director of the Congressional Budget Office, delivered the best explication of the marriage penalty in a 1996 report, then took time to review her work with me. While at the Joint Tax Committee Ken Kies unveiled the intricacies of the Earned Income Credit. Grover Norquist and Jim Lucier of Americans for Tax Reform helped to cull tax outrages.

The firm H&R Block bravely endured my attentions through the winter of 1997–1998. Thanks there go to Linda McDougall, the late Rusty Wallower, and the inimitable Henry Bloch himself. Walt Riker of McDonald's took the time to travel to Florida to introduce me to the Rodriguez family. Thanks to McDonald's and the Rodriguezes for opening my eyes to the burdens of the payroll tax.

The Social Security Administration hosted me for a day. Larry DeWitt talked me through the history of the SSA. The Internal Revenue Service also gave me time: thanks much to Frank Keith and his colleagues, who faithfully responded to my calls and faxes.

Larry Lindsey of the American Enterprise Institute taught me much, as did Diana Furchtgott-Roth. Barbara Ledeen and her Independent Women's Forum lent their support numerous times.

Many people contributed to the schools chapter. They include Diane Ravitch and Mary Butz, neighbors and inspiriters. Chester Finn gave me the keys to school finance. I learned a lot in Ohio, where I was hosted by Dave Zanotti of the Ohio Round Table, the Brennans, and Bert Holt, the light of Ohio school reform. From Vermont, John McLaughry, Jeff Wennberg, Walt Freed, Jeff Pascoe, and Peter Teachout of Vermont Law School kept me posted on the state's school wars. Special thanks to Mary Barrosse, who took the time to tell me her story.

In New York, Mark Hoenig of Weil, Gotshal and Manges explained the intricacies of charitable giving. Dave Schoenbrod of New York Law School pondered the machinations of the greedy hand with me over several pleasant lunches. Ann Thomas and Richard C. H. Beck, Dave's colleagues, enlightened me on the marriage penalty.

The Urban Institute's tax guru, Gene Steuerle, generously lent time. Thanks to his friend Carla Rollandini for her insights into the personalities of accountants.

This project owes a big debt to the Heritage Foundation, which sustained me with a Bradley fellowship so I could take time off from my work at *The Wall Street Journal.* Ed Feulner and Adam Meyerson were unstintingly supportive. Special thanks to Bill Beach for his guidance.

The Hoover Institution at Stanford University gave me a chance to study Proposition 13 in close detail. I'm grateful to John Raisian, Tom Henriksen, and Wendy Minkin, who took me in as a guest. Robert Barro, Ed Lazear, and Rita Ricardo-Campbell all taught me much while I was there. John Cogan, a great editor, read parts of the book. Thanks too to Mike Boskin, Dennis Bark, and Alvin Rabushka for their support.

The Manhattan Institute gave me the wherewithal to study taxes on the East Coast. Many thanks to Richard Gilder and Roger Hertog, and to Larry Mone and Mabel Weill. Thanks to Howard Mittelmark for his fine suggestions.

I owe a debt to the editors at Random House, who from the beginning showed enthusiasm for this strange project. Jon Karp is a wonderful editor. My agent, David Chalfant, and his colleagues, Susan Lohman and Meghan Sercombe, proved their loyalty numerous times.

Big thanks are due to my colleagues at *The Wall Street Jour-*

nal, who tolerated my absence and sustained me through this project. Carol Muller and Bruce Levy helped on the research. Tom Herman, *The Wall Street Journal*'s tax columnist, batted tax topics around with me dozens of times. Special thanks to George Melloan, David Asman, Melanie Kirkpatrick, James Taranto, Max Boot, and Daniel Henninger, who edited the articles and editorials I produced while learning the tax beat. Erich Eichman lent his ear. I feel enormous gratitude to Robert Bartley, editor of *The Wall Street Journal* and tax teacher. *The Greedy Hand* is merely the most recent of the outpourings provoked by his silences.

Finally I thank my extraordinary family. My mother and sister kept me going although they didn't share my views. My father and brother kept me going because they did. Beatrice Barran managed our household while I was on the top floor typing. My greatest debt is to Seth, Eli, Theodore, and Flora, who supported me and, in their varying ways, injected sanity into the exercise. "But Mommy, who would build the roads?"

Brooklyn, July 1998

Bibliography

Books

Adams, Charles. *For Good and Evil.* Lanham, Md.: Madison Books, 1993.

——. *Those Dirty Rotten Taxes.* New York: Free Press, 1998.

Adams, James Ring. *Secrets of the Tax Revolt.* San Diego, Calif.: Harcourt Brace Jovanovich, 1984.

Arthur Andersen & Co. Societe Cooperative. *A Vision of Grandeur.* Geneva: 1988.

Bartley, Robert L. *The Seven Fat Years and How to Do It Again.* New York: Free Press, 1992.

Bastiat, Frederic. *Economic Harmonies.* Irvington-on-Hudson, N.Y.: Foundation for Economic Education, 1996.

——. *Economic Sophisms.* Irvington-on-Hudson, N.Y.: Foundation for Economic Education, 1996.

——. *Selected Essays on Political Economy.* Irvington-on-Hudson, N.Y.: Foundation for Economic Education, 1995.

Beito, David T. *Taxpayers in Revolt.* Chapel Hill: University of North Carolina Press, 1989.

Bernstein, Peter W., ed. *The Ernst & Young Tax Saver's Guide 1998.* New York: John Wiley, 1998.

Birnbaum, Jeffrey H., and Alan S. Murray. *Showdown at Gucci Gulch.* New York: Random House, 1987.

Bloch, Henry, with Michael Shook. *H&R Block's Tax Relief.* Kansas City, Mo.: Andrews and McMeel, 1995.

Bradford, David F. *Distributional Analysis of Tax Policy.* Washington, D.C.: The AEI Press, 1995.

Brookhiser, Richard. *Founding Father: Rediscovering George Washington.* New York: Simon & Schuster, 1996.

Brooks, John. *Business Adventures: Twelve Classic Tales from the Worlds of Wall Street and the Modern Corporation.* New York: Weybright and Talley, 1969.

———. *Once in Golconda: A True Drama of Wall Street, 1920–1938.* New York: Harper & Row, 1969.

———. *Showing Off in America.* Boston: Little, Brown, 1981.

Brown, Karen B., and Mary Louise Fellows. *Taxing America.* New York: New York University Press, 1996.

Brownlee, W. Elliot. *Federal Taxation in America.* Washington: Woodrow Wilson Center Press, 1996.

———. *Funding the Modern American State, 1941–1995.* Washington: Woodrow Wilson Center Press, 1996.

Buchanan, James M., and Gordon Tullock. *The Calculus of Consent.* Ann Arbor, Mich.: University of Michigan Press, 1962.

Buchanan, James M. *Economics.* College Station: Texas A&M University Press, 1987.

Bureau of the Budget. *The United States at War: Development and Administration of the War Program by the Federal Government.* New York: Da Capo, 1972.

Coopers & Lybrand. *Tax Reform Act of 1986.* Washington: Coopers & Lybrand (U.S.A.), 1986.

Cowell, Frank A. *Cheating the Government.* Cambridge, Mass.: MIT Press, 1990.

Crouch, Holmes F. *Being Self-Employed.* Saratoga, Calif.: Allyear Tax Guides, 1998.

Davenport, Charles, ed. *Selected Readings on Tax Policy.* Arlington, Va.: Tax Analysts, 1997.

Davis, Shelley L. *Unbridled Power: Inside the Secret Culture of the IRS.* New York: Harper Audio, 1997.

Dicks, J. W., Charles Smith, Jr., and James L. Paris. *The 100 Best Investments for Your Retirement.* Holbrook, Mass.: Adams Media, 1996.

Dionne, E. J., Jr. *Why Americans Hate Politics.* New York: Simon & Schuster, 1991.

Dolan, Len and Daria. *The Smart Money Family Financial Planner.* New York: Berkley Books, 1992.

Doris, Lillian, ed. *The American Way in Taxation: Internal Revenue, 1862–1963.* Englewood Cliffs, N.J.: Prentice-Hall, 1963.

Edelman, Ric. *The New Rules of Money.* New York: HarperCollins, 1998.

Edwards, Lee. *The Power of Ideas.* Ottawa, Ill.: Jameson Books, 1997.

Eisenstein, Louis. *The Ideologies of Taxation.* New York: Ronald Press, 1961.

Engeman, Thomas S., Edward J. Erler, and Thomas B. Hofeller, eds. *The Federalist Concordance.* Chicago: University of Chicago Press, 1988.

Ferrara, Peter, and Michael Tanner. *A New Deal for Social Security.* Washington: Cato Institute, 1998.

Fisher, Glenn W. *The Worst Tax? A History of the Property Tax in America.* Lawrence, Kan.: University Press of Kansas, 1996.

Fleenor, Patrick, ed. *Facts & Figures: Our Government Finance,* 31st Edition. Washington: Tax Foundation, 1997.

Forsythe, Dall W. *Taxation and Political Change in the Young Nation, 1781–1833.* New York: Columbia University Press, 1977.

Franklin, Benjamin. *Essays on General Politics, Commerce and Political Economy.* 1836. Reprint, New York: Augustus M. Kelley, 1971.

Friedman, Milton. *Capitalism and Freedom.* Chicago: University of Chicago Press, 1962.

———. *Money Mischief.* New York: Harcourt Brace Jovanovich, 1992.

Friedman, Milton and Rose. D. *Two Lucky People: Memoirs.* Chicago: University of Chicago Press, 1998.

Galbraith, John Kenneth. *The Affluent Society.* Boston: Houghton Mifflin, 1984.

Gilder, George. *Wealth and Poverty.* New York: Basic Books, 1981.

Gordon, John Steele. *Hamilton's Blessing.* New York: Walker and Company, 1997.

Graetz, Michael J. *The Decline (and Fall?) of the Income Tax.* New York: W. W. Norton, 1997.

———. *Federal Income Taxation.* Westbury, N.Y.: Foundation Press, 1988.

Greenberg, Stanley B. *Middle Class Dreams.* New Haven: Yale University Press, 1995.

Gross, Martin L. *The Tax Racket.* New York: Ballantine Books, 1995.

A Guide to the 104th Congress. Washington: The LTV Corp., 1996.

Hamilton, Alexander, James Madison, and John Jay. *The Federalist Papers.* 1787–1788. Reprint, New York: New American Library, 1961. Also audio script, Nashville, Tenn.: Knowledge Products, 1986.

H&R Block Tax Services Inc. *1988, 1996 and 1998 Income Tax Guides.* New York: Simon & Schuster, 1997.

———. *Basic Income Tax Course.* 1997.

Hanke, Thomas, and Norbert Walter. *Der Euro—Kurs auf die Zukunft.* Frankfurt: Campus Verlag, 1997.

Hannon, Kerry. *10 Minute Guide to Retirement for Women.* New York: Simon & Schuster Macmillan, 1996.

Hayek, Friedrich A. von. *The Essence of Hayek.* Edited by Chiaki Nishiyama and Kurt R. Leube. Stanford, Calif.: Hoover Institution Press, 1984.

———. *The Road to Serfdom.* 1944. Reprint, Chicago: University of Chicago Press, 1976.

Hazlitt, Henry. *Economics in One Lesson.* New York: Crown, 1979.

Heilbroner, Robert L. *The Worldly Philosophers.* New York: Simon & Schuster, 1972.

Hodous, Robert P. *Let's Really Change Taxes.* Charlottesville, Va.: Robert P. Houdous, 1997.

Howard, A. E. Dick, ed. *The United States Constitution: Roots, Rights and Responsibilities.* Washington: Smithsonian Institution Press, 1992.

Howard, Christopher. *The Hidden Welfare State.* Princeton, N.J.: Princeton University Press, 1997.

Howard, Michael. *Strategic Deception in the Second World War.* New York: W. W. Norton, 1995.

Hultberg, Nelson. *Why We Must Abolish the Income Tax and the IRS.* Dallas: AFR Publications, 1996.

Internal Revenue Service. *Annual Report of the Commissioner of Internal Revenue.* Washington: Department of the Treasury, 1952.

——, Shelley Davis, ed. *IRS Historical Factbook: A Chronology, 1646–1992.* Washington: Department of the Treasury, 1992.

——. *Taxpayer Advocate's Annual Report to Congress.* Washington: Department of the Treasury, FY1996 and FY1997.

——. *Older Americans' Tax Guide.* Washington: Department of the Treasury, 1997.

——. *Miscellaneous Deductions.* Washington: Department of the Treasury, 1997.

Jefferson, Thomas, *Autobiography, Notes on the State of Virginia, Public and Private Papers, Addresses, Letters.* Reprint, New York: Library of America, 1984.

Joint Committee on Taxation. *Present Law and Analysis Relating to Individual Effective Marginal Tax Rates.* Washington: U.S. Government Printing Office, Feb. 4, 1998.

——. *Tax Modeling Project and 1997 Tax Symposium Papers.* Washington: U.S. Government Printing Office, Nov. 20, 1997.

Jones, Carolyn C. "Mass-based Income Taxation: Creating a Taxpaying Culture, 1940–1952." (In Brownlee, W. Elliot, *Funding the Modern American State, 1941–1995*).

Kaplan, Martin, and Naomi Weiss. *What the IRS Doesn't Want You to Know.* New York: Villard, 1996.

Kellems, Vivien. *Toil, Taxes and Trouble.* New York: E. P. Dutton, 1952.

Kennon, Donald R., and Rebecca M. Rogers. *The Committee on Ways and Means: A Bicentennial History, 1889–1989.* Washington: U.S. Government Printing Office, 1989.

Kirk, Russell, ed. *The Portable Conservative Reader.* New York: Viking Penguin, 1982.

Korn, Donald J. *Audit-Proof Tax Shelters.* Englewood Cliffs, N.J.: Prentice-Hall, 1993.

Kotlikoff, Laurence J. *Generational Accounting.* New York: Macmillan, 1992.

Kozol, Jonathan. *Savage Inequalities: Children in America's Schools.* New York: Crown, 1991.

Lebergott, Stanley. *Consumer Expenditures.* Princeton, N.J.: Princeton University Press, 1996.

————. *Pursuing Happiness.* Princeton, N.J.: Princeton University Press, 1993.

Levine, Arthur, and Jeanette S. Cureton. *When Hope and Fear Collide.* San Francisco: Jossey-Bass, 1998.

Lieberman, Jethro K. *The Enduring Constitution.* St. Paul: West Publishing, 1987.

Lieberman, Myron. *Public Education: An Autopsy.* Cambridge, Mass.: Harvard University Press, 1993.

Love, Philip. *Andrew W. Mellon: The Man and His Work.* Baltimore, Md.: F. Heath Coggins, 1929.

Maier, Pauline. *American Scripture: Making the Declaration of Independence.* New York: Alfred A. Knopf, 1997.

McCaffery, Edward J. *Taxing Women.* Chicago: University of Chicago Press, 1997.

McElvaine, Robert S. *The Great Depression.* New York: Random House, 1993.

Melloan, George, and Joan. *The Carter Economy.* New York: John Wiley, 1978.

Mellon, Andrew W. *Taxation: The People's Business.* New York: Macmillan, 1924.

Mill, John Stuart. *Principles of Political Economy.* 1848. Reprint, Fairfield, N.J.: Augustus M. Kelley, 1987.

Miller, Roger LeRoy. *Economics Today.* New York: HarperCollins, 1991.

Miner, Brad. *The Concise Conservative Encyclopedia.* New York: Simon & Schuster, 1996.

Moody, Scott, ed. *Facts and Figures on Government Finance.* Washington. Tax Foundation, 1998.

Mueller, Dennis C., ed. *Perspectives on Public Choice.* Cambridge, England: Cambridge University Press, 1997.

O'Hearn, Taylor W., ed. *The Constitution of the United States with Explanations.* Shreveport, La.: APH, 1986.

Paine, Thomas. *Collected Writings.* Reprint, New York: Library of America, 1995.

Paine, Thomas. *Common Sense* (1776) and *The Crisis* (1792). Reprint, Garden City, N.Y.: Doubleday, 1960.

Paul, Randolph E. *Taxation for Prosperity.* Indianapolis: Bobbs-Merrill, 1947.

————. *Taxation in the United States.* Boston: Little, Brown, 1954.

Pechman, Joseph A. *Federal Tax Policy.* Washington: Brookings Institution, 1971.

Penner, Rudolph G. *Taxing the Family.* Washington: AEI Press, 1983.

Pollack, Sheldon D. *The Failure of U.S. Tax Policy.* University Park, Pa.: Pennsylvania State University Press, 1996.

Ratner, Sidney. *Taxation and Democracy in America.* New York: Farrar, Straus and Giroux, 1980.

Resnick, Judy. *I've Been Rich. I've Been Poor. Rich Is Better.* New York: Golden Books, 1998.

Ruml, Beardsley. *Tomorrow's Business.* New York: Farrar & Rinehart, 1945.

Samuelson, Paul A. *Economics.* New York: McGraw-Hill, 1973.

Scalia, Antonin. *A Matter of Interpretation.* Princeton, N.J.: Princeton University Press, 1997.

Sears, David O., and Jack Citrin. *Tax Revolt: Something for Nothing in California.* Cambridge, Mass.: Harvard University Press, 1982.

Seligman, Edwin R. A. *Essays in Taxation.* New York: Augustus M. Kelley, 1969.

————. *The Income Tax.* New York: Augustus M. Kelley, 1970.

Senate Committee on Finance. *Practices and Procedures of the Internal Revenue Service (Hearings Before the Committee on Finance).* Washington: U.S. Government Printing Office, 1997.

Shannon, David S. *The Great Depression.* Englewood Cliffs, N.J.: Prentice-Hall, 1960.

Shughart, William F. II, ed. *Taxing Choice.* New Brunswick, N.J.: Transaction Publishers, 1997.

Slemrod, Joel, and Jon Bakija. *Taxing Ourselves.* Cambridge, Mass.: MIT Press, 1996.

Smiley, Jane. *A Thousand Acres.* New York: Ballantine Books, 1991.

Smith, Adam. *The Wealth of Nations.* 1776. Reprint, New York: The Modern Library, 1937.

Smith, James Morton, ed. *The Republic of Letters: Vol. 1 (1776–1790).* New York: W. W. Norton, 1995.

Stanley, Thomas J., and William D. Danko. *The Millionaire Next Door.* Atlanta: Longstreet Press, 1996.

Stern, Philip M. *The Great Treasury Raid.* New York: Random House, 1964.

Steuerle, C. Eugene, and Jon M. Bakija. *Retooling Social Security for the 21st Century.* Washington: Urban Institute Press, 1994.

Steuerle, C. Eugene. *The Tax Decade.* Washington: Urban Institute Press, 1992.

Supreme Court. *Pollock v. Farmers' Loan and Trust Co. Hyde v. Continental Trust Co.* Washington: U.S. Government, April and May, 1895.

Thau, Richard D., and Jay S. Heflin, eds. *Generations Apart: Xers vs. Boomers vs. the Elderly.* Amherst, N.Y.: Prometheus Books, 1997.

Tocqueville, Alexis de. *Democracy in America.* Reeve, Brown, Bradley, eds. New York: Alfred Knopf, 1945.

Tocqueville, Alexis de. *The Old Regime and the French Revolution.* New York: Doubleday, 1983.

Tyson, Eric, and David J. Silverman. *Taxes for Dummies.* Foster City, Calif.: IDG Books, 1998.

Ward, John William. *Andrew Jackson: Symbol for an Age.* London: Oxford University Press, 1953.

Weatherford, Jack. *The History of Money.* New York: Crown, 1997.

Wiegold, C. Frederic, ed. *The Wall Street Journal Lifetime Guide to Money.* New York: Hyperion, 1997.

Wright, Chester W. *Economic History of the United States.* New York: McGraw-Hill, 1941.

Vickrey, William. *Agenda for Progressive Taxation.* New York: Ronald Press, 1947.

Other Sources

"Toward a Family Centered Theory of Taxation," by Allan Carlson, *The Family in America, Vol. 12, No. 1.* 1998. The Howard Center for Family, Religion and Society.

"Clintons Earned $1 Million in 1996, Including Royalties," by David Stout, *The New York Times,* April 14, 1997.

"Complicating the Federal Tax Code: A Look at the Alternative Minimum Tax" by Gary Robbins, Aldona Robbins. Institute for Policy Innovation, 1998.

David Boyter and Angela M. Boyter v. Commissioner of Internal Revenue, U.S. Court of Appeals Fourth Circuit, No. 80-1792.

"Fine Print in Gains Tax Exclusion," by Jay Romano, *The New York Times,* January 18, 1998.

The Firm, movie from the novel by John Grisham, Paramount, 1993.

"For Better or for Worse: Marriage and the Federal Income Tax," Congressional Budget Office, June 1997.

"The Honeymooners' Lost Episodes: Income Tax," MPI Home Video.

"How a Tax Law Helps Insure a Scarcity of Programmers," by David Cay Johnston, *The New York Times,* April 27, 1998.

"IRS Angers Family of Pan Am Crash Victim," by Robert D. Hershey, Jr., *The New York Times,* December 22, 1994.

"IRS Wants $6 Million from Damages Family Has Never Seen," Cable News Network, December 23, 1994.

"Rein in the Revenue Hounds," by Amity Shlaes, *The Wall Street Journal,* March 24, 1998.

"She's Too Over-taxed to Keep Jackie's Gem," by Charles Sussman, *New York Post,* February 28, 1998.

Social Security Manual, Globe Communications Corp., 1996 edition.

Tax Quotes, Tax Analysts 1997 Calendar, Tax Analysts, 1997.

"Ten Tax-Friendly Retirement Towns," by Carolyn Rice, *Where to Retire* magazine, Summer, 1998.

TurboTax Deluxe, federal return tax year 1997, Quicken compact disc.

"U.S. Tax Bite on Foreign Luxury," by Noelle Knox, *The New York Times,* May 22, 1998.

Index

About the Author

AMITY SHLAES is the youngest member of the *Wall Street Journal*'s editorial board, where she is an editorialist on tax policy. Her writing has also been published in *Commentary* and *The New Yorker*. She is the author of *Germany: The Empire Within*. A magna cum laude graduate of Yale University, she lives in New York City with her husband, Seth Lipsky, and their three children.

About the Type

This book was set in Old Style 7. Old Style faces
are based on sixteenth- and seventeenth-century faces
of the Dutch, English, and French designers. They are
characterized by definite strokes and bracketed serifs.
The original Old Style is based on an English old face.
Old Style 7 is smaller-appearing than the original,
and has much less contrast between thick and thin.
Old Style was cut for the Mergenthaler Linotype
Company in 1905, which also had variations of the
face for distribution.